WORLD'S GREATEST

Christmas

Activity
Book

For KIDS

W9-BEG-970

World's Greatest Christmas

Christmas

Activity Book

For KIDS

KEN SAVE

BARBOUR PUBLISHING

The World's Greatest Christmas Activity Book for Kids © 2008 by Barbour Publishing, Inc.
Winter Fun © 2002 by Barbour Publishing, Inc.
The Best Present Ever © 2002 by Barbour Publishing, Inc.
Jesus is Born © 2002 by Barbour Publishing, Inc.
Christmas Around the World © 2002 by Barbour Publishing, Inc.

ISBN 978-1-61626-865-7

All rights reserved. No part of this publication may be reproduced or transmitted in any form or by any means without written permission of the publisher.

Scripture taken from the HOLY BIBLE, NEW INTERNATIONAL VERSION®. NIV®. Copyright © 1973, 1978, 1984 by International Bible Society. Used by permission of Zondervan. All rights reserved.

Published by Barbour Publishing, Inc., P.O. Box 719, Uhrichsville, Ohio 44683 www.barbourbooks.com

Our mission is to publish and distribute inspirational products offering exceptional value and biblical encouragement to the masses.

Member of the
Evangelical Christian
Publishers Association

Printed in the United States of America.
Bethany Press International, Bloomington, MN 55438; August 2012; D10003503

CAN YOU PICTURE IT?

THE PICTURES ARE YOUR CLUES. USE THE CIRCLED LETTERS TO
COMPLETE THE PUZZLE BELOW.

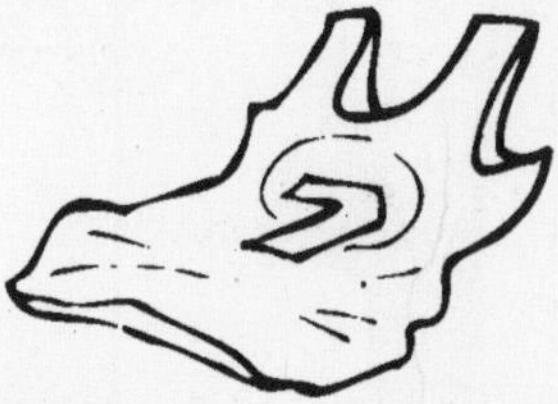

Juggle

rose

donkey

party hat

mouse trap

Jerseys

THEY WILL BE THE PARENTS OF JESUS. WHO ARE THEY?

Joseph & mary

5

FIND THE FOUR

COMPLETE THE PUZZLE BELOW BY CROSSING OUT EVERY
LETTER THAT APPEARS AT LEAST FOUR TIMES. USE THE
REMAINING LETTERS TO COMPLETE THE SENTENCE.

```
B J C T C T S I W Y N
N X O W C P D X H L Z
J ■ L R K U P N V V B
P I Q D W B K G E I J
D Q O H ■ M I S Z R Q
S G A E V O Q L K F U
G U S P F J N F ███ T
Z K Z E H W X F ███ C D
E V L U H B G T ███ O X
```

MARY AND JOSEPH PLAN TO _____.

6

DON'T LEAVE IT SCRAMBLED!

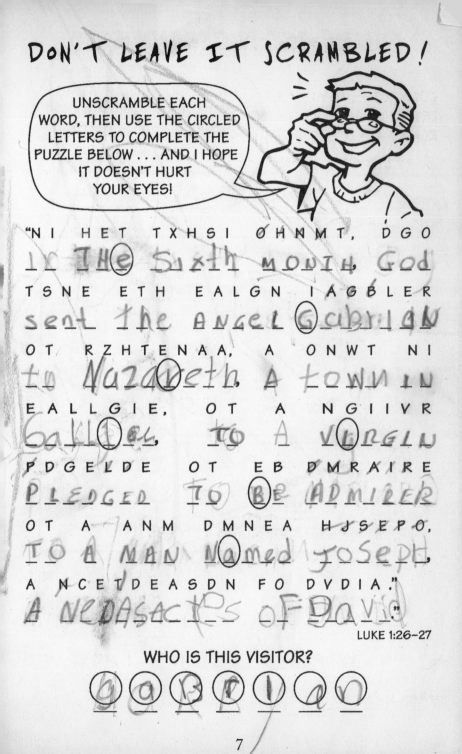

UNSCRAMBLE EACH WORD, THEN USE THE CIRCLED LETTERS TO COMPLETE THE PUZZLE BELOW . . . AND I HOPE IT DOESN'T HURT YOUR EYES!

"NI HET TXHSI ØHMMT, DGO
IN THE SIXTH MONTH, God
TSNE ETH EALGN IAGBLER
sent the angel Gabriel
OT RZHTENAA, A ONWT NI
to Nazareth, A town in
EALLGIE, OT A NGIIVR
Galilee, to A virgin
PDGELDE OT EB DMRAIRE
Pledged to be admired
OT A ANM DMNEA HJSEPO,
to a man named Joseph,
A NCETDEASDN FO DVDIA."
A nedasactes of David."

LUKE 1:26–27

WHO IS THIS VISITOR?

Gabriel

7

WHERE ARE THOSE VOWELS?

YOU'RE GOING TO HAVE TO CONCENTRATE FOR THIS ONE! VOWELS ARE HIDDEN IN THE PICTURE BELOW. YOU WILL NEED THEM TO COMPLETE THE PUZZLE.

"TH_ ANG_L W_NT T_ H_R _ND S__D, 'GR__T_NGS, Y__ WH_ _R_ H_GHLY F_V_R_D! TH_ L_RD _S W_TH Y__.'"

LUKE 1:28

8

LETTER CLUES

TO DECODE THIS MESSAGE FROM GOD, YOU'LL NEED TO TAKE THE LETTER FROM EACH NUMBERED CLUE AND MATCH IT TO THE NUMBERED SPACE IN THE PUZZLE BELOW.

1. LOOK FOR THIS IN BOTH *RAFT* AND *HORSE*.

   _____

2. THIS ONE IS SEEN ONCE IN *RUG* AND TWICE IN *JUGGLE*.

   _____

3. THIS LETTER IS FOUND TWICE IN *NONE* AND *NUN*.

   _____

4. BEGINS THE WORD *HOT* AND ENDS THE WORD *TOUGH*.

   _____

5. BEGINS THE WORD *OPEN* AND FOUND SECOND IN *ROPE*.

   _____

6. THIS LETTER IS FOUND ONCE IN *YELLOW* AND *BABY*.

   _____

7. THIS LETTER CAN BE FOUND IN *WHEEL* AND *SWIM*.

   _____

8. CAN BE SEEN THREE TIMES IN *TATTLE* AND ONCE IN *TOY*.

   _____

9. *HOLY* HAS ONE BUT *HOLLY* HAS TWO.

   _____

10. THIS LETTER IS FOUND IN *GIRLS* BUT NOT *GIRL*.

    _____

"'YOU WILL BE WITH C E I __ D AND __ IVE BIRTH TO
        7   4 9   2
A S __ N, AND __ OU A __ E __ O GIVE HIM THE __ AME
    5   6   1   8   3
JE __ US.'"
   10

LUKE 1:31

PICTURE CLUES

THE PICTURES ARE YOUR ONLY CLUES TO COMPLETING THIS CROSSWORD. THIS IS A BIT OF A BRAIN TEASER.

UP OR DOWN?

UNSCRAMBLE THE WORDS, THEN IT'S UP TO YOU TO FIND WHERE EACH WORD GOES. WE PUT A FEW LETTERS IN TO HELP.

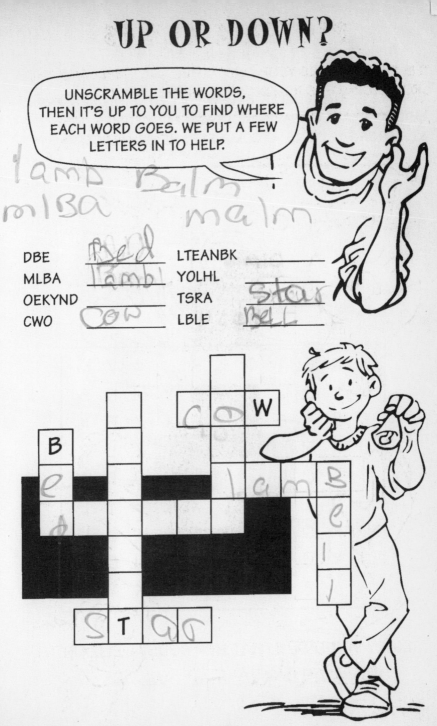

DBE	Bed	LTEANBK	
MLBA	lamb	YOLHL	
OEKYND		TSRA	star
CWO	cow	LBLE	bell

11

FIND THE FOUR

COMPLETE THE PUZZLE BELOW BY CROSSING OUT EVERY LETTER THAT APPEARS AT LEAST FOUR TIMES. USE THE REMAINING LETTERS TO COMPLETE THE SENTENCE.

```
H K F T O R P J Y V M
N V Q Z C W G V M E S
P B A S V Q U T Z E K
U X M           Z L R
G E O           O P W
S N T J F G X Z B Y F
D R Q I K R S A W J U
J Y U P N M O G N Q B
A T F W E B X A K Y X
```

MARY FINDS OUT THAT HER COUSIN, ELIZABETH, WILL ALSO HAVE A _b_ _a_ _b_ _ _ _ _ .

12

TRAVELLIN' RHYMES

THIS IS A GREAT GAME TO PLAY AS YOU TRAVEL. YOU'LL NEED SOMEONE TO PLAY IT WITH, THOUGH, LIKE YOUR BROTHER OR SISTER OR FRIENDS.

BELOW IS A LIST OF WORD PAIRS THAT RHYME WITH EACH OTHER. YOUR JOB IS TO CALL OUT THE WORDS AND HAVE THE PLAYERS COME UP WITH THE SILLIEST RHYMES. WRITE THE BEST ON THE SPACES BELOW.

HAIR, BEAR   TACK, BACK
JUICE, LOOSE   SMILE, TRIAL
RUN, BUN   BIKE, LIKE
ICE, TWICE   ARROW, SPARROW
BALL, HALL   DARK, PARK

_____

_____

_____

_____

_____

_____

_____

_____

PICTURE MAKER

YOU MAKE THE PICTURE. DRAW THE IMAGE FROM EACH FRAME AT THE TOP IN THE FRAME BELOW WITH THE MATCHING NUMBER.

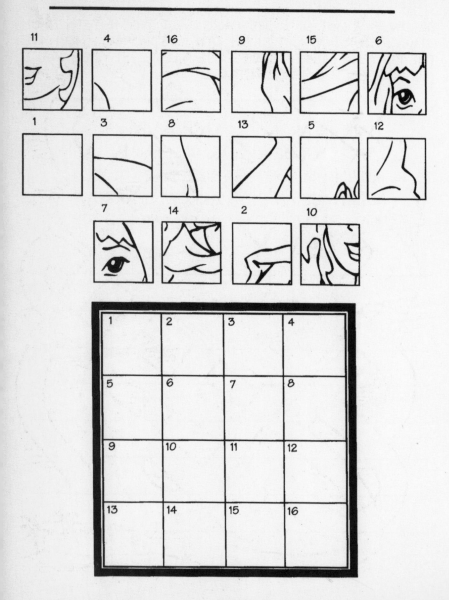

LET'S MAZE AROUND

MARY'S GOING TO VISIT HER COUSIN, ELIZABETH. CAN YOU HELP HER FIND HER WAY?

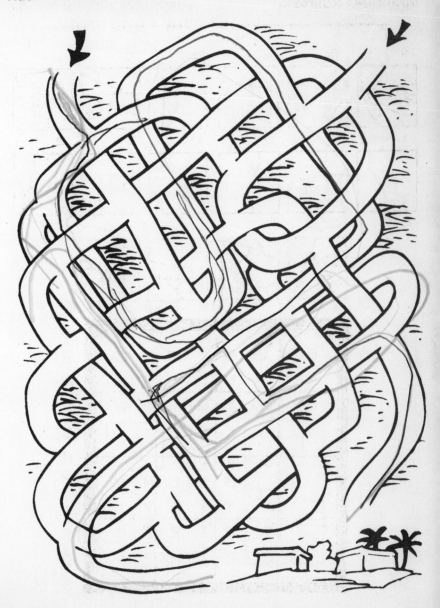

CAN YOU FIND THE WORDS?

ALL THESE
WORDS ARE HIDDEN IN
THE PUZZLE BELOW.
HAVE FUN!

TREE
KING
MAGI
GALILEE
STAR

INN
JUDEA
CHILD
HEROD
CAMEL

```
              Y  J
              J  K
S D W K G F L R K F I W G P
T C H I L D H N U N D C
A A S H N B P W S G H A
X F R D T N B L D J B M
Q G D P S V H I O W V E
H N       L E F     N L
E W       J U S     C H
R B     G U L N B R P
O F     Y T D V I W I
D R     R T R E E G F
T D     R T H P A T D
Z F G A L I L E E M A O S M
```

16

WHERE ARE THOSE VOWELS?

YOU'RE GOING TO HAVE TO CONCENTRATE FOR THIS ONE! VOWELS ARE HIDDEN IN THE PICTURE BELOW. YOU WILL NEED THEM TO COMPLETE THE PUZZLE.

"WHEN ELIZABETH HEARD MARY'S GR___T_NG, TH_ BABY L___P_D IN HER W_MB, AND ELIZABETH WAS F_LL_D WITH THE H_LY SP_R_T."

LUKE 1:41

REALLY SILLY STORIES

YOU CAN PLAY THIS GAME BY YOURSELF, BUT IT'S A LOT MORE FUN TO PLAY WITH OTHERS.

ASK EACH PLAYER TO CALL OUT THE KIND OF WORD INDICATED IN EACH SPACE—A NOUN OR ADJECTIVE OR ADVERB, FOR EXAMPLE—AND PLACE THAT WORD IN THE APPROPRIATE SPACE. DO NOT TELL ANYONE WHAT THE STORY IS ABOUT—IT'S MORE FUN THAT WAY!

BELOW YOU'LL FIND A DESCRIPTION OF WHAT VERBS, NOUNS, ADJECTIVES, ADVERBS, ETC., ARE—JUST IN CASE YOU NEED A LITTLE HELP.

<u>VERB:</u> AN ACTION WORD, LIKE *WALK, RUN,* OR *FLY.* MAY BE *WALKED, RAN,* OR *FLEW,* IF <u>PAST TENSE</u> IS CALLED FOR.

<u>ADVERB:</u> MODIFIES A VERB AND USUALLY ENDS IN "LY." *SLOWLY* AND *CAREFULLY* ARE A COUPLE OF EXAMPLES.

<u>NOUN:</u> A PERSON, PLACE, OR THING, LIKE *BOY, BOAT,* OR *CAR.*

<u>ADJECTIVE:</u> DESCRIBES SOMEONE OR SOMETHING. *DIRTY, SILLY,* AND *BIG* ARE A FEW EXAMPLES.

<u>PLACE:</u> COULD BE A *COUNTRY* OR *CITY,* ETC.

<u>PLURAL:</u> MORE THAN ONE ITEM, SUCH AS *GIRLS* IS THE PLURAL OF *GIRL.*

NOW MOVE ON TO THE FOLLOWING PAGE TO PLAY THIS REALLY SILLY GAME!

REALLY SILLY STORIES

DON'T LOOK AT THE STORY BELOW. INSTEAD, FILL IN THE BLANKS IN THE LIST BELOW WITH THE REQUIRED WORDS. THEN FILL IN THE BLANKS IN THE STORY AND GET READY TO LAUGH UNCONTROLLABLY!

PLURAL NOUN _Girls_
ADJECTIVE _silly_
ADJECTIVE _dirty_
NAME _molly_
NOUN _bus_
VERB (PAST TENSE) _____
NOUN _____
ADJECTIVE _____
VERB ENDING IN "ING" _____
VERB (PAST TENSE) _____
ADJECTIVE _____
ADVERB _____

VERB (PAST TENSE) _____
NAME _____
VERB (PAST TENSE) _____
ADJECTIVE _____
VERB _____
NOUN _____
NAME OF SEASON _____
NOUN _____
VERB _____
VERB (PAST TENSE) _____
VERB (PAST TENSE) _____
NOUN _____

THE GRADE SIX _____ AT CENTRAL _____ SCHOOL
              PLURAL NOUN   ADJECTIVE

WERE LOOKING _____ TO THEIR TRIP TO _____
              ADJECTIVE   NAME

MOUNTAIN. THE _____ HAD FINALLY _____ AND
              NOUN   VERB (PAST TENSE)

_____ WAS _____ FOR _____. THEY _____
NOUN   ADJECTIVE   VERB — "ING"   VERB (PAST TENSE)

ON SPENDING THE _____ DAY _____ AND ALL EAGERLY
              ADJECTIVE   ADVERB

_____ THE FUN AHEAD. _____, HOWEVER, WAS
VERB (PAST TENSE)   NAME

_____ ABOUT _____ THING; WOULD HE STILL
VERB (PAST TENSE)   ADJECTIVE

_____ THE _____ TO PERFORM IN THE _____
VERB   NOUN   NAME OF SEASON

PLAY AT HIS _____, LATER IN THE EVENING? HE DIDN'T
           NOUN

_____ TO MISS IT AND _____ HE HADN'T _____ ON
VERB   VERB (PAST TENSE)   VERB (PAST TENSE)

TOO MUCH FOR ONE _____.
              NOUN

DON'T LEAVE IT SCRAMBLED!

UNSCRAMBLE EACH WORD, THEN USE THE CIRCLED LETTERS TO COMPLETE THE PUZZLE BELOW ... AND I HOPE IT DOESN'T HURT YOUR EYES!

"SCBEAEU SHEOJP RHE DSBHNUA

"Be̲c̲a̲u̲s̲e̲ Joseph her husband

SWA A OGRIUHSTE ANM DAN

w̲a̲s̲ a R̲i̲g̲h̲t̲e̲o̲u̲s̲ m̲a̲n̲ and

IDD TNO TANW OT PSXOEE RHE

D̲I̲D̲ N̲o̲t̲ w̲a̲n̲t̲ to E̲x̲p̲o̲s̲e̲ Her

OT UCLPIB AIGERDSC, EH DHA NI

t̲o̲ P̲u̲b̲l̲i̲c̲ D̲i̲s̲g̲r̲a̲c̲e̲, he had I̲N̲

DMNI OT RVOECDI EHR YUQLITE."

m̲i̲n̲d̲ T̲o̲ D̲i̲v̲o̲r̲c̲e̲ her Q̲u̲i̲e̲t̲l̲Y"

MATTHEW 1:19

WHAT DID JOSEPH PLAN TO DO ABOUT THE WEDDING?

◯ ◯ ◯ ◯ ◯ ◯

20

it's a Mystery

THIS IS A GREAT GAME TO PLAY AS YOU TRAVEL. YOU'LL NEED SOMEONE TO PLAY IT WITH, THOUGH, LIKE YOUR BROTHER OR SISTER OR FRIENDS.

BELOW IS A LIST OF PHRASES THAT NEED TO BE COMPLETED. SHOW THIS PUZZLE TO EACH PLAYER, WHO PICKS A LETTER TO FILL IN THE BLANKS, AND THEN HAS TEN SECONDS TO GUESS THE PHRASE. MOVE ON TO EACH PLAYER UNTIL THE MYSTERY IS SOLVED! AS THE HOST OF THIS GAME, YOU GET TO CHECK OUT THE SOLUTION FROM THE ANSWER PAGES AT THE BACK (IF YOU NEED TO)!

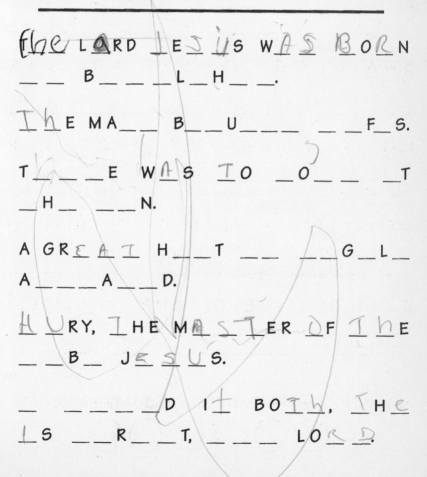

T h e L O R D J E S U S W A S B O R N

_ _ B _ _ _ L _ H _ _ .

T h E M A _ _ _ B _ _ U _ _ _ _ _ F _ S.

T _ _ _ E W A S T O _ O _ _ _ T

_ H _ _ _ N.

A G R E A T H _ _ _ T _ _ _ _ G _ L _

A _ _ _ _ A _ _ D.

H _ R Y, T H E M A S T E R O F T h E

_ _ B _ J E S U S.

_ _ _ _ _ _ D I t B O T h, T h E

I S _ _ R _ _ T, _ _ _ L O R D.

21

CAN YOU PICTURE IT?

THE PICTURES ARE YOUR CLUES. USE THE CIRCLED LETTERS TO COMPLETE THE PUZZLE BELOW.

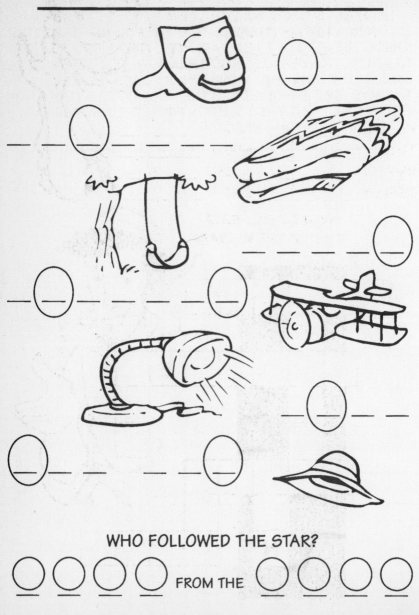

WHO FOLLOWED THE STAR?

○ ○ ○ ○ FROM THE ○ ○ ○ ○
_ _ _ _ _ _ _ _

22

UP OR DOWN?

UNSCRAMBLE THE WORDS, THEN IT'S UP TO YOU TO FIND WHERE EACH WORD GOES. WE PUT A FEW LETTERS IN TO HELP.

HSJEPO _____   ATS _____

TTNE _____   NDE _____

RMREDIA _____   SJESU _____

TEBALS _____   SNO _____

WHAT CAN I SAY?
I *LOVE* THE WOMAN!

WHO, WHAT, WHERE

THIS IS A GREAT GAME TO PLAY AS YOU TRAVEL. YOU'LL NEED SOMEONE TO PLAY IT WITH, THOUGH, LIKE YOUR BROTHER OR SISTER OR FRIENDS.

BELOW IS A LIST OF QUESTIONS THAT NEED A "WHO, WHAT, OR WHERE" ANSWER. EACH PLAYER HAS TEN SECONDS TO ANSWER. AS THE HOST OF THIS GAME, YOU GET TO CHECK OUT THE SOLUTION FROM THE ANSWER PAGES AT THE BACK (IF YOU NEED TO)!

THIS YOUNG GIRL WAS VISITED BY AN ANGEL WITH GOOD NEWS. *WHO* WAS SHE? _____

LUKE 1:26–33

THIS RULER WAS VERY AFRAID OF THE BIRTH OF JESUS CHRIST. *WHO* WAS HE? _____

MATTHEW 2:3

MARY TRAVELLED WITH JOSEPH TO THIS PROVINCE TO GIVE BIRTH. *WHERE* WERE THEY? _____

LUKE 2:4

THIS PLACE WAS FULL, FORCING THE YOUNG COUPLE TO GO ELSEWHERE. *WHAT* WAS IT? _____

LUKE 2:7

HAVING BEEN WARNED, JOSEPH TOOK HIS FAMILY HERE TO LIVE. *WHERE* ARE THEY? _____

MATTHEW 2:13–15

THIS LED MAGI FROM THE EAST TO THE BIRTHPLACE OF CHRIST. *WHAT* WAS IT? _____

MATTHEW 2:9

PICTURE CLUES

THE PICTURES ARE YOUR ONLY CLUES TO COMPLETING THIS CROSSWORD. THIS IS A BIT OF A BRAIN TEASER.

ALL JUMBLED UP

HEY . . . THIS ONE WILL BE FUN!
FIND THE OPPOSITE OF EACH WORD,
THEN USE THE CIRCLED LETTERS TO
COMPLETE THE PUZZLE BELOW.

MOTHER _ _ _ _ ⦿ _

SUN ⦿ _ _ _

PEN _ ⦿ _ _ ⦿

DOG _ _ ⦿

DAY _ _ _ ⦿

COLD ⦿ _ _

STRAIGHT ⦿ _ _ _

TIRED _ _ _ _ ⦿

WHERE DID THE MIRACLE BEGIN?

◯ ◯ ◯ ◯ ◯ ◯ ◯ ◯ ◯

26

PICTURE MAKER

YOU MAKE THE PICTURE. DRAW THE IMAGE FROM EACH FRAME AT THE TOP IN THE FRAME BELOW WITH THE MATCHING NUMBER.

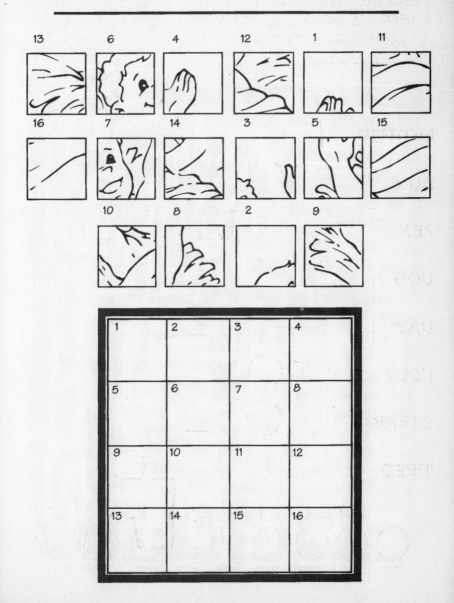

LET'S MAZE AROUND

WE ARE IN BETHLEHEM, AND MARY AND JOSEPH NEED HELP
FINDING A PLACE FOR HER TO GIVE BIRTH. CAN YOU HELP?

JUST A REGULAR OLD CROSSWORD!

ACROSS

1. HEAVENLY HOST
2. A SPECIAL BABY
3. PLACE FOR ANIMALS
4. CRIB FOR JESUS
5. RIDDEN BY MARY
6. A FALSE GOD

DOWN

1. JOSEPH'S HOMETOWN
2. PROVINCE OF ISRAEL
3. THEY CARE FOR SHEEP
4. LARGE GROUP OF SHEEP
5. THE CREATOR
6. ANCIENT MOTEL

WHERE ARE THOSE VOWELS?

YOU'RE GOING TO HAVE TO CONCENTRATE FOR THIS ONE! VOWELS ARE HIDDEN IN THE PICTURE BELOW. YOU WILL NEED THEM TO COMPLETE THE PUZZLE.

"SH_ WR_PP_D H_M _N
CL_THS _ND PL_C_D H_M
_N _ M_NG_R, B_C_ _S_
TH_R_ W_S N_ R_ _ M
F_R TH_M _N TH_ _NN."

LUKE 2:7

30

LETTER CLUES

TO DECODE THIS MESSAGE FROM GOD, YOU'LL NEED TO TAKE
THE LETTER FROM EACH NUMBERED CLUE AND MATCH IT TO
THE NUMBERED SPACE IN THE PUZZLE BELOW.

1. THIS LETTER BEGINS *HAIR* AND ENDS *ROUGH*.
   _____

2. FOUND SECOND TO LAST IN BOTH *LOVE* AND *LEAVE*.
   _____

3. FOUND ONCE IN *CRUMB* AND TWICE IN *ACCEPT*.
   _____

4. THIS ONE'S TWICE IN *EFFECT* BUT ONCE IN *FAIR*.
   _____

5. YOU'LL FIND THIS ONE IN *BEST* BUT NOT IN *BUST*.
   _____

6. YOU'LL FIND THIS TWICE IN *BABY* AND ONCE IN *BOAT*.
   _____

7. THIS LETTER BEGINS *GOAT* AND ENDS *JOG*.
   _____

"AND T _ _ R _   W _ R _   S _ _ P _ _ RDS
       1 5   5   5   5   1 5   1 5
LI _ IN _ OUT IN T _ _   _ I _ LDS N _ AR _ Y,
   2   7   1 5   4 5   5   6
K _ _ PIN _   WAT _ _   _ O _ _ R   T _ _ IR
  5 5   7   3 1   2 5   1 5
_ LO _ KS AT NI _ _ T."
4   3   7 1

LUKE 2:8

31

CAN YOU FIND THE WORDS?

ALL THESE WORDS ARE HIDDEN IN THE PUZZLE BELOW. HAVE FUN!

BASKET

CHURCH

TEMPLE

SUNDAY

FLOCK

JOSEPH

BIBLE

STAR

MANGER

MAGI

FIND THE FOUR

COMPLETE THE PUZZLE BELOW BY CROSSING OUT EVERY LETTER THAT APPEARS AT LEAST FOUR TIMES. USE THE REMAINING LETTERS TO COMPLETE THE SENTENCE.

WELL . . . *I* COULD USE AN ANGEL RIGHT ABOUT NOW!

Math ÷

M	V	X	K	M	Q	W	R	I	Y
H	G	B	Z	S	C	C	K	E	X
R	P	J	B	F	Z	Q	V	H	R
C	T	Q	W	H	■	Z	C	D	K
U	K	D	J	U	I	J	S	V	T
W	O	M	Z	O	X	M	D	O	Y
S	N	U	P	Y	L	P	Y	B	F
F	P	X	O	D	R	T	F	Q	V
I	W	T	I	A	J	S	U	H	B

AN __ __ __ __ __ APPEARS TO THE SHEPHERDS.

UP OR DOWN?

UNSCRAMBLE THE WORDS, THEN IT'S UP TO YOU TO FIND WHERE EACH WORD GOES. WE PUT A FEW LETTERS IN TO HELP.

ISHHGTE	_____	WCAHT	_____
ONTW	_____	SHTO	_____
GYLRO	_____	DLGA	_____
VLNYEEAH	_____	ISH	_____
DLRO	_____	AEHRT	_____
HNEOS	_____	ERATH	_____

WHO, WHAT, WHERE

THIS IS A GREAT GAME TO PLAY AS YOU TRAVEL. YOU'LL NEED SOMEONE TO PLAY IT WITH, THOUGH, LIKE YOUR BROTHER OR SISTER OR FRIENDS.

BELOW IS A LIST OF QUESTIONS THAT NEED A "WHO, WHAT, OR WHERE" ANSWER. EACH PLAYER HAS TEN SECONDS TO ANSWER. AS THE HOST OF THIS GAME, YOU GET TO CHECK OUT THE SOLUTION FROM THE ANSWER PAGES AT THE BACK (IF YOU NEED TO)!

SHEPHERDS WERE AT WORK, LOOKING AFTER THEIR SHEEP. *WHERE* WERE THEY? _____

LUKE 2:8

SUDDENLY, SOMETHING SHONE ALL AROUND THEM. *WHAT* WAS IT? _____

LUKE 2:9

HE BROUGHT THEM *GOOD NEWS OF GREAT JOY* FOR ALL PEOPLE. *WHO* WAS HE? _____

LUKE 2:10

A SAVIOR HAD BEEN BORN WHO WAS CHRIST, THE LORD. *WHERE* WAS HE BORN? _____

LUKE 2:11

ALL GLORY WAS GIVEN TO HIM BY THE ANGELS AND ALL MEN. *WHO* WAS HE? _____

LUKE 2:14

HE HAD NO BED, BUT THEY FOUND A PLACE TO LAY HIM DOWN. *WHAT* WAS IT? _____

LUKE 2:12

PEACE WAS GIVEN TO THEM ON WHOM RESTED THE FAVOR OF GOD. *WHO* WERE THEY? _____

LUKE 2:14

PICTURE MAKER

YOU MAKE THE PICTURE. DRAW THE IMAGE FROM EACH FRAME AT THE TOP IN THE FRAME BELOW WITH THE MATCHING NUMBER.

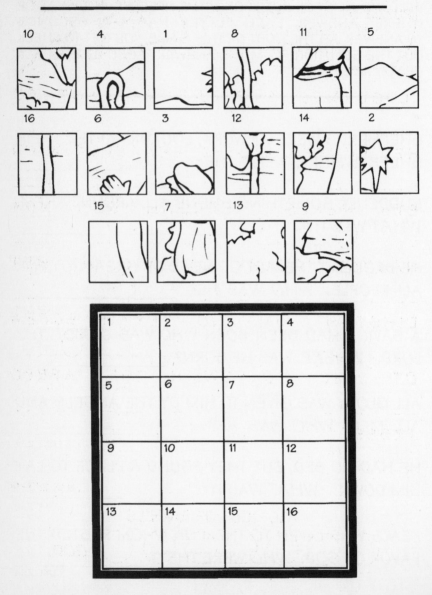

DON'T LEAVE IT SCRAMBLED!

UNSCRAMBLE EACH WORD, THEN USE THE CIRCLED LETTERS TO COMPLETE THE PUZZLE BELOW . . . AND I HOPE IT DOESN'T HURT YOUR EYES!

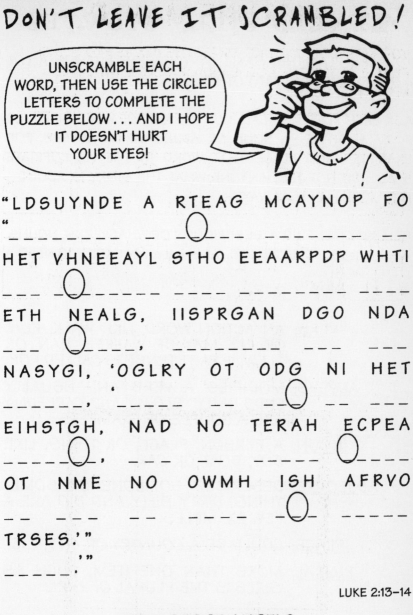

"LDSUYNDE   A   RTEAG   MCAYNOP   FO

"_ _ _ _ _ _ _ _   _   _ Ⓞ _ _ _   _ _ _ _ _ _ _   _ _

HET   VHNEEAYL   STHO   EEAARPDP   WHTI

_ _ _   _ Ⓞ _ _ _ _ _ _   _ _ _ _   _ _ _ _ _ _ _ _   _ _ _ _

ETH   NEALG,   IISPRGAN   DGO   NDA

_ _ _   _ Ⓞ _ _ _,   _ _ _ _ _ _ _ _   _ _ _   _ _ _

NASYGI,   'OGLRY   OT   ODG   NI   HET

_ _ _ _ _ _,   '_ Ⓞ _ _ _   _ _   _ _ _   _ _   _ _ _

EIHSTGH,   NAD   NO   TERAH   ECPEA

_ _ _ _ _ Ⓞ _,   _ _ _   _ _   _ _ _ Ⓞ _   _ _ _ _ _

OT   NME   NO   OWMH   ISH   AFRVO

_ _   _ _ _   _ _   _ _ _ _   _ Ⓞ _   _ _ _ _ _

TRSES.'"

_ _ _ _ _.'"

LUKE 2:13–14

THE HOST OF ANGELS

Ⓞ Ⓞ Ⓞ Ⓞ Ⓞ Ⓞ Ⓞ GOD.

37

REALLY SILLY STORIES

YOU *CAN* PLAY THIS GAME BY YOURSELF, BUT IT'S A LOT MORE FUN TO PLAY WITH OTHERS.

ASK EACH PLAYER TO CALL OUT THE KIND OF WORD INDICATED IN EACH SPACE—A NOUN OR ADJECTIVE OR ADVERB, FOR EXAMPLE—AND PLACE THAT WORD IN THE APPROPRIATE SPACE. DO NOT TELL ANYONE WHAT THE STORY IS ABOUT— IT'S MORE FUN THAT WAY!

BELOW YOU'LL FIND A DESCRIPTION OF WHAT VERBS, NOUNS, ADJECTIVES, ADVERBS, ETC., ARE—JUST IN CASE YOU NEED A LITTLE HELP.

VERB: AN ACTION WORD, LIKE *WALK*, *RUN*, OR *FLY*. MAY BE *WALKED*, *RAN*, OR *FLEW*, IF <u>PAST TENSE</u> IS CALLED FOR.

ADVERB: MODIFIES A VERB AND USUALLY ENDS IN "LY." *SLOWLY* AND *CAREFULLY* ARE A COUPLE OF EXAMPLES.

NOUN: A PERSON, PLACE, OR THING, LIKE *BOY*, *BOAT*, OR *CAR*.

ADJECTIVE: DESCRIBES SOMEONE OR SOME-THING. *DIRTY*, *SILLY*, AND *BIG* ARE A FEW EXAMPLES.

PLACE: COULD BE A *COUNTRY* OR *CITY*, ETC.

PLURAL: MORE THAN ONE ITEM, SUCH AS *GIRLS* IS THE PLURAL OF *GIRL*.

NOW MOVE ON TO THE FOLLOWING PAGE TO PLAY THIS REALLY SILLY GAME!

REALLY SILLY STORIES

DON'T LOOK AT THE STORY BELOW. INSTEAD, FILL IN THE
BLANKS IN THE LIST BELOW WITH THE REQUIRED WORDS.
THEN FILL IN THE BLANKS IN THE STORY AND GET READY TO
LAUGH UNCONTROLLABLY!

PLURAL NOUN —————————
NOUN _____
PLURAL NOUN _____
VERB _____
NOUN _____
NOUN _____
ADJECTIVE _____
PLURAL NOUN _____
VERB ENDING IN "ING" _____
TIME OF DAY _____
PLURAL NOUN _____
PLURAL NOUN _____
PLURAL NOUN _____
VERB (PAST TENSE) _____

VERB _____
ADVERB _____
NOUN _____
PLURAL NOUN _____
NOUN _____
NOUN _____
VERB (PAST TENSE) _____
PLURAL NOUN _____
VERB _____
NOUN _____
NOUN _____
VERB ENDING IN "ING" _____
ADJECTIVE _____

THE _____ FROM THE SUNDAY _mom_ CLASS WERE
    PLURAL NOUN   NOUN

ALL IN THEIR _____ AND COULD HARDLY _____
          PLURAL NOUN   VERB

THEIR _____. THE _____ WAS ABOUT TO START!
     NOUN   PLURAL NOUN

FOR THE _____ TWO _____, THEY HAD BEEN
       ADJECTIVE   PLURAL NOUN

_____ FOR THIS SPECIAL _____, BUILDING
 VERB—"ING"   TIME OF DAY

_____, SEWING _____, AND LEARNING THEIR
 PLURAL NOUN   PLURAL NOUN

_____. THEY WERE _____ IN THEIR RESOLVE
 PLURAL NOUN   VERB (PAST TENSE)

TO _____ THIS THE BEST PLAY ANYONE HAD _____
  VERB   ADVERB

SEEN. FINALLY, THE _____ ARRIVED. THE
                    NOUN

_____ DIMMED AND A _____ FELL OVER THE
 PLURAL NOUN   NOUN

_____. THE CURTAIN _____ AND THE _____
 NOUN   VERB (PAST TENSE)   PLURAL NOUN

WERE GRATIFIED TO _____ THE EXPRESSIONS OF
               VERB

_____ FROM EVERYONE IN THE _____. THIS WAS
 NOUN   NOUN

_____ TO BE A _____ NIGHT!
 VERB-"ING"   ADJECTIVE

39

JUST A REGULAR OLD CROSSWORD!

ACROSS

1. JESUS WAS BORN THERE
2. GIVE LIGHT
3. COMPANY OF ANGELS
4. TOWN OF _____
5. THE ANGELS WERE DOING IT

DOWN

1. BORN TO MARY
2. A CARPENTER
3. VERY HIGH
4. VERY AFRAID
5. HE WOULD BRING THIS

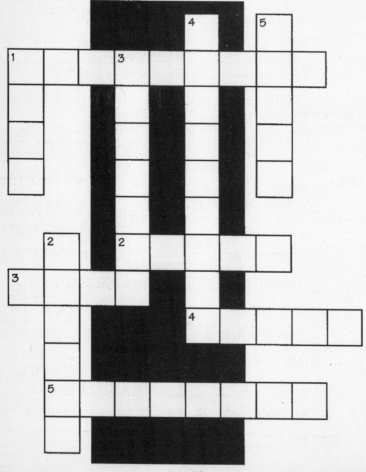

TRAVELLIN' RHYMES

THIS IS A GREAT GAME TO PLAY AS YOU TRAVEL. YOU'LL NEED SOMEONE TO PLAY IT WITH, THOUGH, LIKE YOUR BROTHER OR SISTER OR FRIENDS.

BELOW IS A LIST OF WORD PAIRS THAT RHYME WITH EACH OTHER. YOUR JOB IS TO CALL OUT THE WORDS AND HAVE THE PLAYERS COME UP WITH THE SILLIEST RHYMES. WRITE THE BEST ON THE SPACES BELOW.

TRAVEL, GRAVEL   HEART, START
HOST, COAST   CLEANER, MEANER
SUN, FUN   CAR, STAR
CARE, FAIR   BLOW, GROW
BED, SLED   GREETING, MEETING

_____

_____

_____

_____

_____

_____

_____

_____

_____

_____

FIND THE FOUR

COMPLETE THE PUZZLE BELOW BY CROSSING OUT EVERY LETTER THAT APPEARS AT LEAST FOUR TIMES. USE THE REMAINING LETTERS TO COMPLETE THE SENTENCE.

H	E	A	M	B	S	G	P	H	C
C	K	P	J	G	N	F	L	T	J
I	H	R	Q	T	K	U	E	S	N
P	Q	V	K	I	U	B	Y	G	H
F	B	T	W	F	M	Q	V	W	X
J			Y	X	P	S	Y	A	T
M	X	A	E	Q	O	J	I	N	C
V	Y	X	G	U	W	K	C	U	F
A	W	V	I	M	D	B	E	N	S

AT THE TOP . . .
AT THE TOP!

JESUS IS OUR SAVIOR AND OUR _ _ _ _ _ .

42

UP OR DOWN?

UNSCRAMBLE THE WORDS,
THEN IT'S UP TO YOU TO FIND WHERE
EACH WORD GOES. WE PUT A FEW
LETTERS IN TO HELP.

OIRSHPW _____

RADME _____

RHRYM _____

RTMHEO _____

TOYRNCU _____

PPRHOTE _____

FOR YOU!

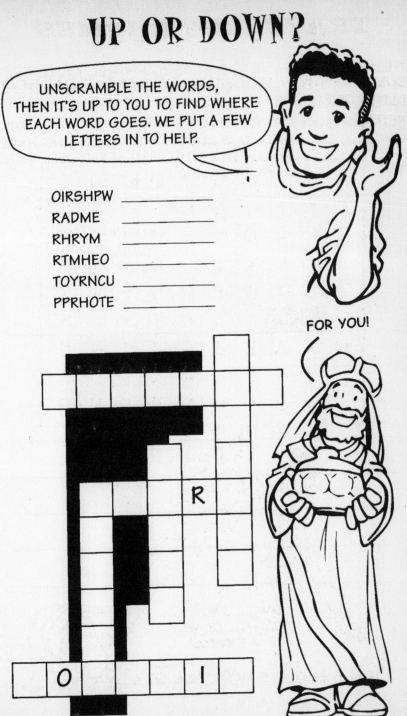

TRAVELLIN' RHYMES

THIS IS A GREAT GAME TO PLAY AS YOU TRAVEL. YOU'LL NEED SOMEONE TO PLAY IT WITH, THOUGH, LIKE YOUR BROTHER OR SISTER OR FRIENDS.

BELOW IS A LIST OF WORD PAIRS THAT RHYME WITH EACH OTHER. YOUR JOB IS TO CALL OUT THE WORDS AND HAVE THE PLAYERS COME UP WITH THE SILLIEST RHYMES. WRITE THE BEST ON THE SPACES BELOW.

MIXTURE, FIXTURE   STRONG, LONG
SALT, MALT   GOOD, HOOD
LAW, SAW   SMILE, WHILE
FEAR, NEAR   STAR, FAR

_____

_____

_____

_____

_____

_____

_____

_____

JUNE... SPOON...
LOON... DUNE...
MOON...

CAN YOU FIND THE WORDS?

ALL THESE WORDS ARE HIDDEN IN THE PUZZLE BELOW. HAVE FUN!

WARNED
DREAM
BOWED
KING
CHILD

MYRRH
TREASURE
GOLD
COUNTRY
REPORT

```
        W D W K
        T A F R
        L H R Z
N B K R F Z V M N E T S K B
G O T R E A S U R E A O I V
C W N E C N O H D F D M N K
J E G O L D R B H R B R G J
D P L J R M T L O Y T E
S S Z Y E J P W R G F A
    H M F A V A T E C H
    W D M R N M P B
    P G A U K B O D
    Z V N O E C O R L G
    R G K C H I L D T W P S
```

CAN YOU PICTURE IT?

THE PICTURES ARE YOUR CLUES. USE THE CIRCLED LETTERS TO
COMPLETE THE PUZZLE BELOW.

WHAT DID THE ANGEL TELL JOSEPH IN HIS DREAM?

LET'S MAZE AROUND

HEROD WANTS TO FIND THE NEWBORN JESUS AND KILL HIM. HELP THE FAMILY ESCAPE TO EGYPT.

PICTURE MAKER

YOU MAKE THE PICTURE. DRAW THE IMAGE FROM EACH FRAME AT THE TOP IN THE FRAME BELOW WITH THE MATCHING NUMBER.

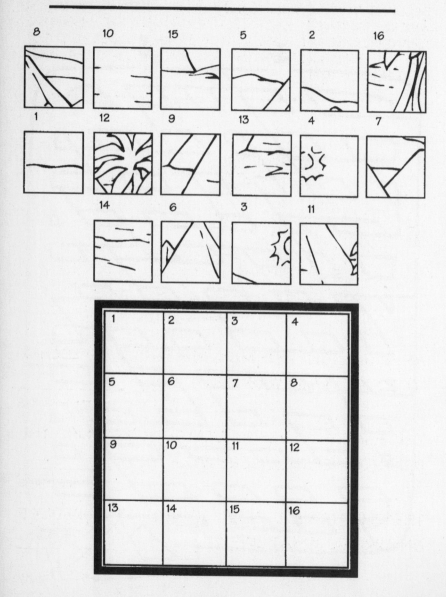

WHO, WHAT, WHERE

THIS IS A GREAT GAME TO PLAY AS YOU TRAVEL. YOU'LL NEED SOMEONE TO PLAY IT WITH, THOUGH, LIKE YOUR BROTHER OR SISTER OR FRIENDS.

BELOW IS A LIST OF QUESTIONS THAT NEED A "WHO, WHAT, OR WHERE" ANSWER. EACH PLAYER HAS TEN SECONDS TO ANSWER. AS THE HOST OF THIS GAME, YOU GET TO CHECK OUT THE SOLUTION FROM THE ANSWER PAGES AT THE BACK (IF YOU NEED TO)!

AN ANGEL TOLD THIS MAN, IN A DREAM, TO ESCAPE TO EGYPT. *WHO* WAS HE? _____

MATTHEW 2:13

THE FAMILY OF JESUS STAYED HERE UNTIL THE DEATH OF HEROD. *WHERE* WERE THEY? _____

MATTHEW 2:14–15

THEY MIGHT HAVE SEEN SOMETHING INCREDIBLE ON ARRIVAL. *WHAT* WAS IT? _____

FIND THE FOUR

COMPLETE THE PUZZLE BELOW BY CROSSING OUT EVERY LETTER THAT APPEARS AT LEAST FOUR TIMES. USE THE REMAINING LETTERS TO COMPLETE THE SENTENCE.

WOW! WHAT A STORY... DON'T YA THINK?

YEAH!

```
M B L F T J W M V O
I E V C S A P U G Q
K T W N Q X Y N X J
L G J Z I Z L ■ A Y
C S X B Z F Q Z C B
P N R Y K T N P U G
A V M Q F S G Y X W
U F W L C J B V H M
K I D T P U A I K S
```

AFTER THE DEATH OF _ _ _ _ _ , THE FAMILY OF JESUS RETURNED TO NAZARETH.

PICTURE MAKER

YOU MAKE THE PICTURE. DRAW THE IMAGE FROM EACH FRAME AT THE TOP IN THE FRAME BELOW WITH THE MATCHING NUMBER.

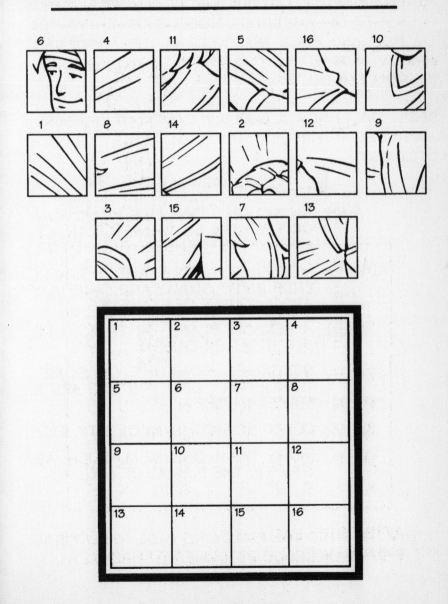

REALLY SILLY STORIES

YOU CAN PLAY THIS GAME BY YOURSELF, BUT IT'S A LOT MORE FUN TO PLAY WITH OTHERS.

ASK EACH PLAYER TO CALL OUT THE KIND OF WORD INDICATED IN EACH SPACE—A NOUN OR ADJECTIVE OR ADVERB, FOR EXAMPLE—AND PLACE THAT WORD IN THE APPROPRIATE SPACE. DO NOT TELL ANYONE WHAT THE STORY IS ABOUT—IT'S MORE FUN THAT WAY!

BELOW YOU'LL FIND A DESCRIPTION OF WHAT VERBS, NOUNS, ADJECTIVES, ADVERBS, ETC., ARE—JUST IN CASE YOU NEED A LITTLE HELP.

VERB: AN ACTION WORD, LIKE *WALK*, *RUN*, OR *FLY*. MAY BE *WALKED*, *RAN*, OR *FLEW*, IF <u>PAST TENSE</u> IS CALLED FOR.

ADVERB: MODIFIES A VERB AND USUALLY ENDS IN "LY." *SLOWLY* AND *CAREFULLY* ARE A COUPLE OF EXAMPLES.

NOUN: A PERSON, PLACE, OR THING, LIKE *BOY*, *BOAT*, OR *CAR*.

ADJECTIVE: DESCRIBES SOMEONE OR SOMETHING. *DIRTY*, *SILLY*, AND *BIG* ARE A FEW EXAMPLES.

PLACE: COULD BE A *COUNTRY* OR *CITY*, ETC.

PLURAL: MORE THAN ONE ITEM, SUCH AS *GIRLS* IS THE PLURAL OF *GIRL*.

NOW MOVE ON TO THE FOLLOWING PAGE TO PLAY THIS REALLY SILLY GAME!

REALLY SILLY STORIES

DON'T LOOK AT THE STORY BELOW. INSTEAD, FILL IN THE BLANKS IN THE LIST BELOW WITH THE REQUIRED WORDS. THEN FILL IN THE BLANKS IN THE STORY AND GET READY TO LAUGH UNCONTROLLABLY!

PLACE _park_

ADJECTIVE _____

VERB (PAST TENSE) _____

ADJECTIVE _____

NOUN _____

PLURAL NOUN _____

ADVERB _____

VERB ENDING IN "ING" _____

NOUN _____

PART OF BUILDING _____

PLURAL NOUN _____

ADJECTIVE _____

VERB _____

ADJECTIVE _____

NOUN _____

PLURAL NOUN _____

NOUN _____

ADJECTIVE _____

NOUN _____

PLURAL NOUN _____

VERB (PAST TENSE) _____

PLURAL NOUN _____

NOUN _____

NAME OF SEASON _____

THE CHRISTMAS PLAY AT _park_ WAS A _____ HIT!
        PLACE   ADJECTIVE

WHY, THEY EVEN _____ A _____ _Daniel_ AND
              VERB (PAST TENSE) ADJECTIVE   NOUN

ALL THE PARENTS AND _____ WERE FULL OF PRAISE
                    PLURAL NOUN

_____. NOW, ALL THE CHILDREN WERE _____
ADVERB

FORWARD TO THE _Oscar_ IN THE MAIN _____. THERE
               NOUN   PART OF BLDG.

WERE _____ FULL OF ALL KINDS OF _____ THINGS TO
     PLURAL NOUN   ADJECTIVE

_____ AND A WHOLE _____ _____ ENTIRELY FOR
VERB   ADJECTIVE   NOUN

_____. IT WAS STILL EARLY IN THE _____
PLURAL NOUN   NOUN

AND THE KIDS WERE _____ WITH GREAT ANTICIPATION
                  ADJECTIVE

FOR THE _____ WHEN THEY WERE TO GIVE THE _____
        NOUN   PLURAL NOUN

THEY HAD _____ ON FOR WEEKS, TO THEIR _____.
         VERB (PAST TENSE)   PLURAL NOUN

AFTER ALL, AS THEY HAD LEARNED IN THE _____, GIVING
                                       NOUN

WAS WHAT _____ WAS ALL ABOUT.
         NAME OF SEASON

WHO, WHAT, WHERE

THIS IS A GREAT GAME TO PLAY AS YOU TRAVEL. YOU'LL NEED SOMEONE TO PLAY IT WITH, THOUGH, LIKE YOUR BROTHER OR SISTER OR FRIENDS.

BELOW IS A LIST OF QUESTIONS THAT NEED A "WHO, WHAT, OR WHERE" ANSWER. EACH PLAYER HAS TEN SECONDS TO ANSWER. AS THE HOST OF THIS GAME, YOU GET TO CHECK OUT THE SOLUTION FROM THE ANSWER PAGES AT THE BACK (IF YOU NEED TO)!

THEY TRAVELLED A *GREAT* DISTANCE TO SEE A NEW-BORN KING. *WHO* WERE THEY? _____

IT IS A MESSAGE OF JOY AND COMES ONCE EVERY YEAR. *WHAT* IS IT? _____

IF THIS KING HAD GOTTEN HIS WAY, THERE WOULD BE NO CHRISTMAS. *WHO* WAS HE? _____

A MIRACULOUS STAR SHONE BRIGHTLY OVER THIS LITTLE TOWN. *WHERE* WAS IT? _____

IT'S ONE WAY WE RE-LIVE THE SPIRIT OF CHRISTMAS WITH LOVED ONES. *WHAT* IS IT? _____

UP OR DOWN?

UNSCRAMBLE THE WORDS, THEN IT'S UP TO YOU TO FIND WHERE EACH WORD GOES. WE PUT A FEW LETTERS IN TO HELP.

GNLEA _____   LKACB _____

MRSISTHAC _____   MIGA _____

_____   EUDAJ _____

YMFALI _____   TGSFI _____

VROSAI _____   LDGA _____

NMGIDKO _____

55

REALLY SILLY STORIES

YOU CAN PLAY THIS GAME BY YOURSELF, BUT IT'S A LOT MORE FUN TO PLAY WITH OTHERS.

ASK EACH PLAYER TO CALL OUT THE KIND OF WORD INDICATED IN EACH SPACE—A NOUN OR ADJECTIVE OR ADVERB, FOR EXAMPLE—AND PLACE THAT WORD IN THE APPROPRIATE SPACE. DO NOT TELL ANYONE WHAT THE STORY IS ABOUT— IT'S MORE FUN THAT WAY!

BELOW YOU'LL FIND A DESCRIPTION OF WHAT VERBS, NOUNS, ADJECTIVES, ADVERBS, ETC., ARE—JUST IN CASE YOU NEED A LITTLE HELP.

<u>VERB</u>: AN ACTION WORD, LIKE *WALK*, *RUN*, OR *FLY*. MAY BE *WALKED*, *RAN*, OR *FLEW*, IF <u>PAST TENSE</u> IS CALLED FOR.

<u>ADVERB</u>: MODIFIES A VERB AND USUALLY ENDS IN "LY." *SLOWLY* AND *CAREFULLY* ARE A COUPLE OF EXAMPLES.

<u>NOUN</u>: A PERSON, PLACE, OR THING, LIKE *BOY*, *BOAT*, OR *CAR*.

<u>ADJECTIVE</u>: DESCRIBES SOMEONE OR SOMETHING. *DIRTY*, *SILLY*, AND *BIG* ARE A FEW EXAMPLES.

<u>PLACE</u>: COULD BE A *COUNTRY* OR *CITY*, ETC.

<u>PLURAL</u>: MORE THAN ONE ITEM, SUCH AS *GIRLS* IS THE PLURAL OF *GIRL*.

NOW MOVE ON TO THE FOLLOWING PAGE TO PLAY THIS REALLY SILLY GAME!

REALLY SILLY STORIES

DON'T LOOK AT THE STORY BELOW. INSTEAD, FILL IN THE BLANKS IN THE LIST BELOW WITH THE REQUIRED WORDS. THEN FILL IN THE BLANKS IN THE STORY AND GET READY TO LAUGH UNCONTROLLABLY!

VERB (PAST TENSE)

_____

VERB _____

NUMBER _____

NAME OF SEASON

_____

VERB (PAST TENSE)

_____

NOUN _____

NOUN _____

VERB ENDING IN "ING"

_____

VERB (PAST TENSE)

_____

PLURAL NOUN _____

VERB (PAST TENSE)

_____

PLURAL NOUN _____

NOUN_____

VERB ENDING IN "ING"

_____

NOUN _____

VERB (PAST TENSE)

_____

NOUN _____

VERB _____

THE DAY THAT MICHELLE _____ HAD FINALLY COME.
                         VERB (PAST TENSE)

SHE COULD NOT _____ OFF ANY LONGER, ESPECIALLY
                    VERB

WHEN THERE WERE ONLY _____ DAYS LEFT UNTIL
                            NUMBER

_____ EVE. SHE HAD JUST _____ HER
NAME OF SEASON   VERB (PAST TENSE)

_____ AND SO, IT WAS OFF TO THE _____ TO
NOUN   NOUN

DO HER CHRISTMAS _____. AS SHE _____
                      VERB—"ING"   VERB (PAST TENSE)

THROUGH THE MAIN ENTRANCE _____, SHE WAS
                               PLURAL NOUN

_____ BY THE _____ AND THE _____, BUT,
VERB (PAST TENSE)   PLURAL NOUN   NOUN

_____ HER _____ AND RESOLVE, SHE
VERB—"ING"   NOUN

_____ INTO THE CRUSHING _____. SHE
VERB (PAST TENSE)   NOUN

PRAYED SHE WOULD _____ THE DAY.
                        VERB

LET'S MAZE AROUND

CHRISTMAS IN A SHOPPING MALL—WHAT A CRAZY PLACE TO BE! HELP THE FAMILY FIND THEIR WAY THROUGH.

TRAVELLIN' RHYMES

THIS IS A GREAT GAME TO PLAY AS YOU TRAVEL. YOU'LL NEED SOMEONE TO PLAY IT WITH, THOUGH, LIKE YOUR BROTHER OR SISTER OR FRIENDS.

BELOW IS A LIST OF WORD PAIRS THAT RHYME WITH EACH OTHER. YOUR JOB IS TO CALL OUT THE WORDS AND HAVE THE PLAYERS COME UP WITH THE SILLIEST RHYMES. WRITE THE BEST ON THE SPACES BELOW.

PRESENT, PHEASANT	LIGHT, MIGHT
DOOR, SNORE	GLASS, GRASS
PLUM, YUM	GLOW, SNOW
FRIEND, LEND	TREE, BEE

_____

_____

_____

_____

_____

_____

_____

_____

CAN YOU PICTURE IT?

THE PICTURES ARE YOUR CLUES. USE THE CIRCLED LETTERS TO COMPLETE THE PUZZLE BELOW.

CHRISTMAS IS ABOUT

◯ ◯ ◯ ◯ ◯ ◯,
‾ ‾ ‾ ‾ ‾ ‾

NOT GETTING.

60

PICTURE CLUES

THE PICTURES ARE YOUR ONLY CLUES TO COMPLETING THIS CROSSWORD. THIS IS A BIT OF A BRAIN TEASER.

FIND THE FOUR

COMPLETE THE PUZZLE BELOW BY CROSSING OUT EVERY LETTER THAT APPEARS AT LEAST FOUR TIMES. USE THE REMAINING LETTERS TO COMPLETE THE SENTENCE.

WHERE'S JESUS?

A	N	B	P	E	R		D	M	J	N
K	Q	U	S	C	Q	X	V	A	L	
M	J	H	W	Y		G	S	H	O	
C	O	V	K		K	W	U	Y	B	
R	X	P	Y	F	X	N	E	K	D	
P	S	Y	C	L	Q	M	A	X	Q	
D	V	I	E	B	J	S	R	H	W	
O	H	N	R	W	V	O	B	L	T	
J	L	A	U	D	P	C	U	M	E	

JESUS IS OUR __ __ __ __ FROM GOD.

CAN YOU FIND THE WORDS?

ALL THESE
WORDS ARE HIDDEN IN
THE PUZZLE BELOW.
HAVE FUN!

CHRISTMAS   SPECIAL
BETHLEHEM   MALL
ANGELS   SHOPPING
STAR   SPENDING
HOLIDAY   GLORY
CONCERT   JESUS

```
        H M W B
      A   N Q K R G
    C O N C E R T P Y
  H L S D G F V S R D H C
  O N J P T E L O T L S M
  L F R E H M L K S A T A J
B I S V F S G Q S M F R L S
K D G R Z L U J T Z V M L P
G A Q W C W S S F K C A R E
J Y P N F Q I Z D K I N L N
D M S T V R J V W C R G T D
  B E T H L E H E M H S P I
    F C M P L P J Q B D C N
      K B H S H O P P I N G
```

63

JUST A REGULAR OLD CROSSWORD!

ACROSS

1. WHERE LOVE DWELLS
2. ACT OF GOD
3. TO ADORN
4. FOR WALKING ON SNOW
5. TO SHINE BRIGHTLY

DOWN

1. LIKE A BROTHER
2. CARING ACT
3. BIND TOGETHER
4. JESUS GIVES IT TO US
5. TO JOIN CLOTH

PICTURE MAKER

YOU MAKE THE PICTURE. DRAW THE IMAGE FROM EACH FRAME AT THE TOP IN THE FRAME BELOW WITH THE MATCHING NUMBER.

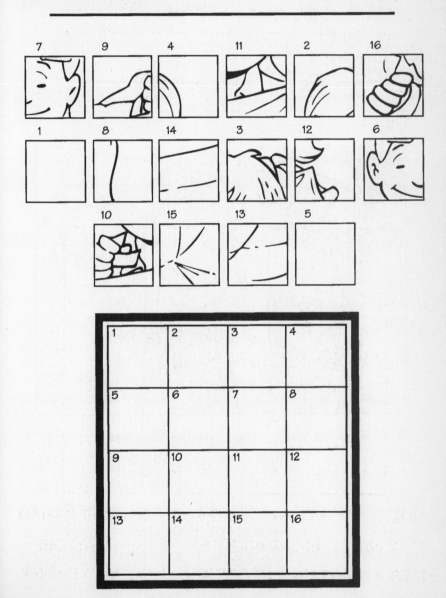

WHERE ARE THOSE VOWELS?

YOU'RE GOING TO HAVE TO CONCENTRATE FOR THIS ONE! VOWELS ARE HIDDEN IN THE PICTURE BELOW. YOU WILL NEED THEM TO COMPLETE THE PUZZLE.

"AFTER JESUS WAS B __ RN __ N BETHLEHEM __ N JUDEA, DUR __ NG THE T __ ME __ F K __ NG HER __ D, MAG __ FR __ M THE EAST CAME T __ JERUSALEM AND ASKED, 'WHERE __ S THE __ NE WH __ HAS BEEN B __ RN K __ NG __ F THE JEWS? WE SAW H __ S STAR __ N THE EAST AND HAVE C __ ME T __ W __ RSH __ P H __ M.'"

MATTHEW 2:1–2

66

LESS SHALL BE FIRST

PLACE THE WORDS BELOW INTO THE PUZZLE ACCORDING TO THE NUMBER OF LETTERS IN EACH WORD, BEGINNING WITH THE WORD THAT HAS THE FEWEST LETTERS. THEN, UNSCRAMBLE THE CIRCLED LETTERS TO COMPLETE THE ANSWER BELOW.

FRIENDS   HOT
GLORY   MOTHER
TRIMMINGS   PRESENTS
BAND   TELEVISION

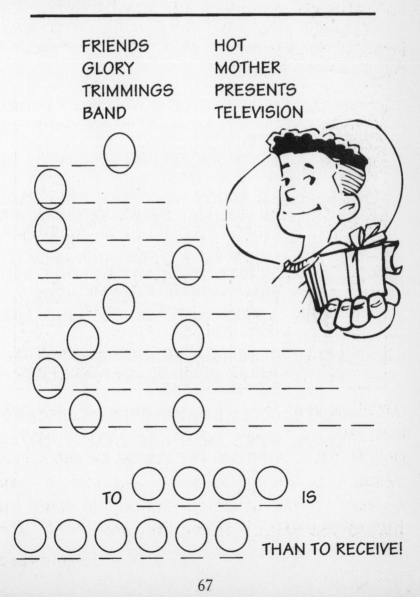

TO _ _ _ _ IS

_ _ _ _ _ THAN TO RECEIVE!

REALLY SILLY STORIES

YOU *CAN* PLAY THIS GAME BY YOURSELF, BUT IT'S A LOT MORE FUN TO PLAY WITH OTHERS.

ASK EACH PLAYER TO CALL OUT THE KIND OF WORD INDICATED IN EACH SPACE—A NOUN OR ADJECTIVE OR ADVERB, FOR EXAMPLE—AND PLACE THAT WORD IN THE APPROPRIATE SPACE. DO NOT TELL ANYONE WHAT THE STORY IS ABOUT— IT'S MORE FUN THAT WAY!

BELOW YOU'LL FIND A DESCRIPTION OF WHAT VERBS, NOUNS, ADJECTIVES, ADVERBS, ETC., ARE—JUST IN CASE YOU NEED A LITTLE HELP.

<u>VERB</u>: AN ACTION WORD, LIKE *WALK*, *RUN*, OR *FLY*. MAY BE *WALKED*, *RAN*, OR *FLEW*, IF <u>PAST TENSE</u> IS CALLED FOR.

<u>ADVERB</u>: MODIFIES A VERB AND USUALLY ENDS IN "LY." *SLOWLY* AND *CAREFULLY* ARE A COUPLE OF EXAMPLES.

<u>NOUN</u>: A PERSON, PLACE, OR THING, LIKE *BOY*, *BOAT*, OR *CAR*.

<u>ADJECTIVE</u>: DESCRIBES SOMEONE OR SOME-THING. *DIRTY*, *SILLY*, AND *BIG* ARE A FEW EXAMPLES.

<u>PLACE</u>: COULD BE A *COUNTRY* OR *CITY*, ETC.

<u>PLURAL</u>: MORE THAN ONE ITEM, SUCH AS *GIRLS* IS THE PLURAL OF *GIRL*.

NOW MOVE ON TO THE FOLLOWING PAGE TO PLAY THIS REALLY SILLY GAME!

REALLY SILLY STORIES

DON'T LOOK AT THE STORY BELOW. INSTEAD, FILL IN THE BLANKS IN THE LIST BELOW WITH THE REQUIRED WORDS. THEN FILL IN THE BLANKS IN THE STORY AND GET READY TO LAUGH UNCONTROLLABLY!

PLURAL NOUN ———————
VERB (PAST TENSE)
———————————
NOUN ———————
ADJECTIVE
NOUN ——————
ADJECTIVE ———————
NOUN ——————
VERB (PAST TENSE)
———————————
PLURAL NOUN ———————
ADVERB ———————
NOUN ——————

VERB ———————————
NOUN ———————————
ADJECTIVE ———————
PLURAL NOUN ———————
ADJECTIVE ———————
NOUN ———————————
NOUN ———————————
NOUN ———————————
NOUN ———————————
NOUN ———————————
TIME OF DAY ———————
PLURAL NOUN ———————
NOUN ———————————

THE ——————— HAD ——————— A WONDERFUL TIME AT

PLURAL NOUN · VERB (PAST TENSE)
——————— THIS CHRISTMAS EVE, BUT WERE ——————— TO BE

NOUN · ADJECTIVE
FINALLY ——————— AFTER A ——————— AND BUSY ———————.

NOUN · ADJECTIVE · NOUN
EVERYONE ——————————— IN, CHANGING INTO THEIR

VERB (PAST TENSE)
———————————, LOOKING ——————— TO THE

PLURAL NOUN · ADVERB
HOT ——————— THEY WOULD ——————— BEFORE THE ———————.

NOUN · VERB · NOUN
MOM AND DAD WERE ESPECIALLY ———————————, AS THEIR

ADJECTIVE
——————————— WERE STILL ——————— AND THEY FOUND

PLURAL NOUN · ADJECTIVE
MUCH ——————— IN THEIR KIDS' ——————— AND

NOUN · NOUN
——————————— ABOUT THE SEASON. THEY WOULD READ

NOUN
FROM THE ———————, THE TRUE ——————— OF THIS ———————

NOUN · NOUN · TIME OF DAY
SO THAT THE ——————————— WOULD KNOW WHAT ALL

PLURAL NOUN
——————— WAS REALLY ABOUT.

NOUN

69

LETTER CLUES

TO DECODE THIS MESSAGE FROM GOD, YOU'LL NEED TO TAKE THE LETTER FROM EACH NUMBERED CLUE AND MATCH IT TO THE NUMBERED SPACE IN THE PUZZLE BELOW.

1. THIS LETTER IS FOUND BOTH IN *BIN* AND IN *TRIM*.

   _____

2. THIS LETTER BEGINS BOTH THE WORDS *DESK* AND *DOG*.

   _____

3. THIS LETTER IS FOUND IN *TALK* BUT NOT IN *WALK*.

   _____

4. THIS LETTER IS FOUND IN *MAZE* BUT NOT IN *HAZE*.

   _____

5. IT APPEARS TWICE IN *BABY* AND ONCE IN *BELL*.

   _____

6. THIS LETTER IS FOUND IN *WING* BUT NOT IN *SING*.

   _____

7. THE SAME LETTER IS FOUND ONCE IN *COARSE* AND IN *SIT*.

   _____

"_H_ __ _ HO_ _HE _ _R_H OF
  3 1 7   1 7   6   3   5 1 3
JE_U_ CHR_____ CA_E A_OU_: H___
   7 7   1 7 3   4   5   3 1 7
_O_HER _ARY _A_ PLE_GE_ _O
 4   4   6 7   2   2   3
_E _ARR_E_ _O JO_EPH, _U_
 5   4 1 2   3   7   5 3
_EFORE _HEY CA_E _OGE_HER,
 5   3   4   3   3
_HE _A_ FOUN_ _O _E ___H
 7   6 7   2   3 5   6 1 3
CH_L_ __HROUGH _HE HOLY
   1 2   3   3
_P_R__."
 7 1 1 3

MATTHEW 1:18

70

WHO, WHAT, WHERE

THIS IS A GREAT GAME TO PLAY AS YOU TRAVEL. YOU'LL NEED SOMEONE TO PLAY IT WITH, THOUGH, LIKE YOUR BROTHER OR SISTER OR FRIENDS.

BELOW IS A LIST OF QUESTIONS THAT NEED A "WHO, WHAT, OR WHERE" ANSWER. EACH PLAYER HAS TEN SECONDS TO ANSWER. AS THE HOST OF THIS GAME, YOU GET TO CHECK OUT THE SOLUTION FROM THE ANSWER PAGES AT THE BACK (IF YOU NEED TO)!

HE ASKED THE MAGI TO RETURN TO HIM, AS HE HAD EVIL IN MIND. *WHO* WAS HE? _____

HE GREW FROM HUMBLE BEGINNINGS TO BE THE SAVIOR OF ALL. *WHO* WAS HE? _____

JESUS' FAMILY RETURNED TO LIVE HERE AFTER EXILE IN EGYPT. *WHERE* WERE THEY?

_____

IT LED THESE MEN OVER A LONG DISTANCE TO SEE A MIRACLE. *WHAT* WAS IT? _____

THROUGH HIS POWER, MARY CONCEIVED A BLESSED CHILD. *WHO* WAS HE? _____

THE MAGI BROUGHT SOMETHING SPECIAL TO JESUS. *WHAT* WAS IT? _____

WHERE ARE THOSE VOWELS?

YOU'RE GOING TO HAVE TO CONCENTRATE FOR THIS ONE! VOWELS ARE HIDDEN IN THE PICTURE BELOW. YOU WILL NEED THEM TO COMPLETE THE PUZZLE.

TH_ B_ST PR_S_NT W_ H_V_ _V_R R_C__V_D _S J_S_S. H_ _S G_D'S GR___T_ST G_FT T_ _S, G_V_N _N L_V_ T_ _LL P_ __PL_.

it's a MYSTERY

THIS IS A GREAT GAME TO PLAY AS YOU TRAVEL. YOU'LL NEED SOMEONE TO PLAY IT WITH, THOUGH, LIKE YOUR BROTHER OR SISTER OR FRIENDS.

BELOW IS A LIST OF PHRASES THAT NEED TO BE COMPLETED. SHOW THIS PUZZLE TO EACH PLAYER, WHO PICKS A LETTER TO FILL IN THE BLANKS, AND THEN HAS TEN SECONDS TO GUESS THE PHRASE. MOVE ON TO EACH PLAYER UNTIL THE MYSTERY IS SOLVED! AS THE HOST OF THIS GAME, YOU GET TO CHECK OUT THE SOLUTION FROM THE ANSWER PAGES AT THE BACK (IF YOU NEED TO)!

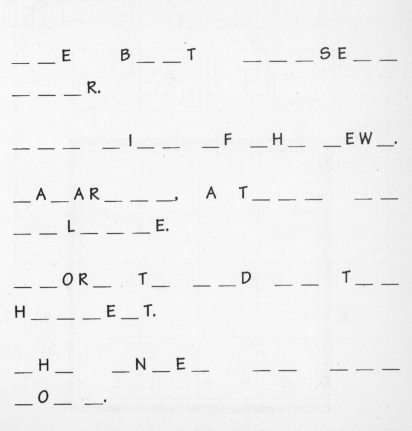

_ _ E   B _ _ T   _ _ _ S E _ _
_ _ _ R.

_ _ _   _ I _ _   _ F _ H _   _ E W _.

_ A _ A R _ _ _,   A   T _ _ _ _   _ _
_ _ L _ _ _ E.

_ _ O R _   T _   _ _ D   _ _   T _ _
H _ _ _ E _ T.

_ H _   _ N _ E _   _ _   _ _ _
_ O _ _.

PICTURE MAKER

YOU MAKE THE PICTURE. DRAW THE IMAGE FROM EACH FRAME AT THE TOP IN THE FRAME BELOW WITH THE MATCHING NUMBER.

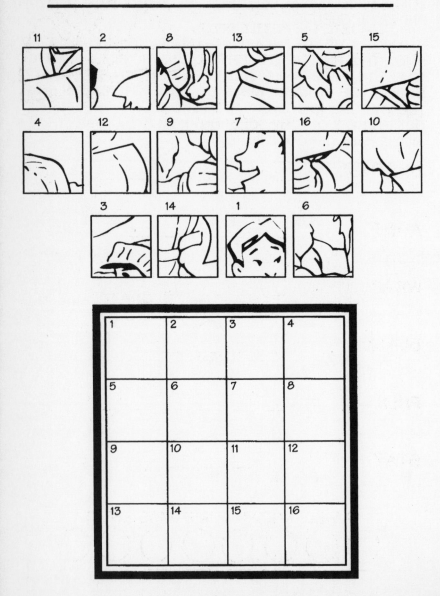

ALL JUMBLED UP

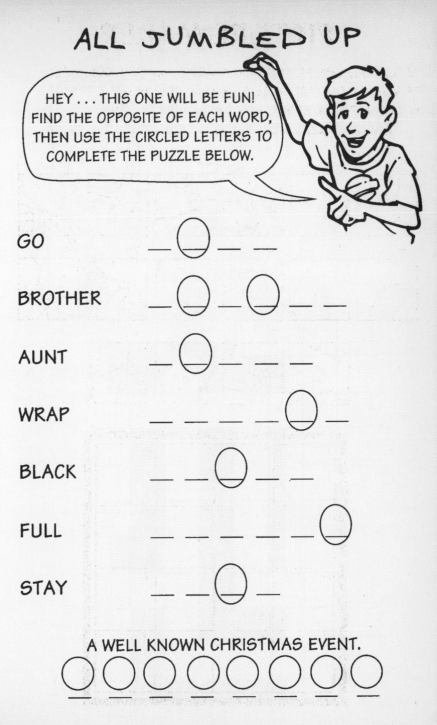

HEY . . . THIS ONE WILL BE FUN!
FIND THE OPPOSITE OF EACH WORD,
THEN USE THE CIRCLED LETTERS TO
COMPLETE THE PUZZLE BELOW.

GO   _ (_) _ _

BROTHER   _ (_) _ (_) _ _

AUNT   _ (_) _ _

WRAP   _ _ _ _ _ (_) _

BLACK   _ _ (_) _ _

FULL   _ _ _ _ (_)

STAY   _ _ (_) _

A WELL KNOWN CHRISTMAS EVENT.

(_) (_) (_) (_) (_) (_) (_) (_)
_ _ _ _ _ _ _ _

75

UP OR DOWN?

UNSCRAMBLE THE WORDS, THEN IT'S UP TO YOU TO FIND WHERE EACH WORD GOES. WE PUT A FEW LETTERS IN TO HELP.

CWHTA _____

EHLBTEMHE _____   NLPA _____

_____   TRAAZHEN _____

OYHL _____   EMRAD _____

TRSA _____   NRWSEA _____

VREALT _____   HEOP _____

FIND THE FOUR

COMPLETE THE PUZZLE BELOW BY CROSSING OUT EVERY LETTER THAT APPEARS AT LEAST FOUR TIMES. USE THE REMAINING LETTERS TO COMPLETE THE SENTENCE.

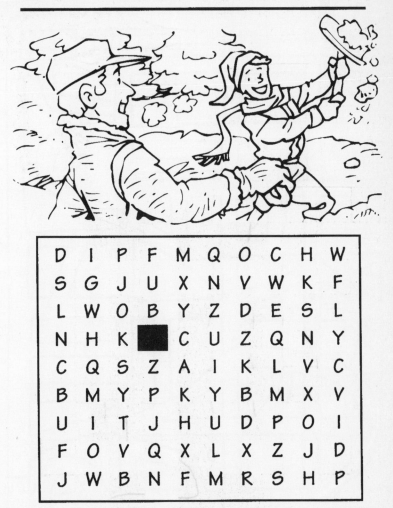

```
D  I  P  F  M  Q  O  C  H  W
S  G  J  U  X  N  V  W  K  F
L  W  O  B  Y  Z  D  E  S  L
N  H  K  ▪  C  U  Z  Q  N  Y
C  Q  S  Z  A  I  K  L  V  C
B  M  Y  P  K  Y  B  M  X  V
U  I  T  J  H  U  D  P  O  I
F  O  V  Q  X  L  X  Z  J  D
J  W  B  N  F  M  R  S  H  P
```

IF EVERYONE PITCHES IN, ALL WILL HAVE A
_ _ _ _ _ DAY!

LET'S MAZE AROUND

THE FAMILY IS HEADING TO GRANDMA'S FOR CHRISTMAS DINNER. HELP THEM GET THROUGH THE BUSY STREETS.

TRAVELLIN' RHYMES

THIS IS A GREAT GAME TO PLAY AS YOU TRAVEL. YOU'LL NEED SOMEONE TO PLAY IT WITH, THOUGH, LIKE YOUR BROTHER OR SISTER OR FRIENDS.

BELOW IS A LIST OF WORD PAIRS THAT RHYME WITH EACH OTHER. YOUR JOB IS TO CALL OUT THE WORDS AND HAVE THE PLAYERS COME UP WITH THE SILLIEST RHYMES. WRITE THE BEST ON THE SPACES BELOW.

STAIR, HAIR	CONE, PHONE
GOOSE, JUICE	SPEAK, BEAK
TRUCK, LUCK	STAND, BAND
PUCK, DUCK	CHAIR, GLARE
RUG, PLUG	GIVING, LIVING

LESS SHALL BE FIRST

PLACE THE WORDS BELOW INTO THE PUZZLE ACCORDING TO THE NUMBER OF LETTERS IN EACH WORD, BEGINNING WITH THE WORD THAT HAS THE FEWEST LETTERS. THEN, UNSCRAMBLE THE CIRCLED LETTERS TO COMPLETE THE ANSWER BELOW.

MIRACLE   SKIING
BREAD   CHOCOLATE
NATIVITY   HOLY
GAB

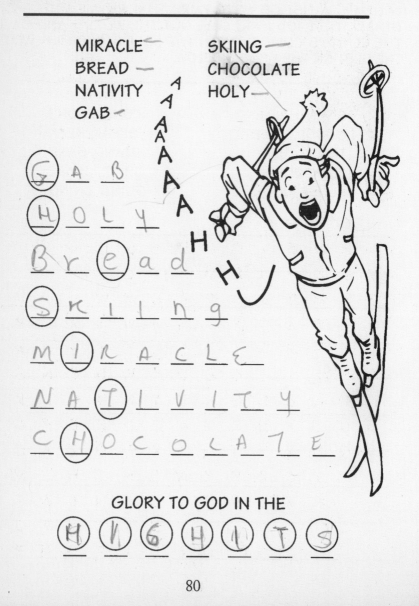

GAB
HOLY
BREAD
SKIING
MIRACLE
NATIVITY
CHOCOLATE

GLORY TO GOD IN THE

H I G H T S

CAN YOU FIND THE WORDS?

ALL THESE
WORDS ARE HIDDEN IN
THE PUZZLE BELOW.
HAVE FUN!

CHILDREN   AUNT
MOTHER   UNCLE
FATHER   GRANDMA
BROTHER   GRANDPA
SISTER   FRIENDS

```
C K G
H N P V D Q R F G
V G R A N D M A T C J
S H M B R L O R U V W M G P
F I S W Q X T H Z N B X R P
L T S F A T H E R Y T S A K
G P L T J C E D K W D F N S
N V K C E G R L Y N B E D R
B U Z X N R H M E D R B P C
Q N Y V J Q I R D O Z A G
  T C Z P R W L N T H J M
  R X L F S I C T H L W T
    D M E H Y B K E Y F B
    J G C Q F D X R S N P
```

JUST A REGULAR OLD CROSSWORD!

ACROSS

1. PURPOSE OF MALL
2. SEED OF A TREE
3. STRINGED INSTRUMENT
4. WINTER VEHICLE
5. JOYOUS EXPRESSION
6. DONE WITH A BOOK

DOWN

1. VOCAL MELODY
2. COLDEST SEASON
3. QUIET MANNER
4. GIVEN TO GOD
5. BETTER THAN POTS
6. CREATOR

LET'S MAZE AROUND

HELP THE MAGI FIND THE BEST ROUTE TO BETHLEHEM.

ALL JUMBLED UP

HEY . . . THIS ONE WILL BE FUN! FIND THE OPPOSITE OF EACH WORD, THEN USE THE CIRCLED LETTERS TO COMPLETE THE PUZZLE BELOW.

FATHER　◯ _ _ _ _ _

SHORT　_ ◯ _ _ _

SICK　_ ◯ _ _ _

WEEDS　◯ _ _ _ _

GRANDMA　_ _ _ ◯ _ _ _

ADD　_ _ _ _ ◯

WHERE WAS THE BABY JESUS BORN?

◯ ◯ ◯ ◯ ◯ ◯

PICTURE MAKER

YOU MAKE THE PICTURE. DRAW THE IMAGE FROM EACH FRAME AT THE TOP IN THE FRAME BELOW WITH THE MATCHING NUMBER.

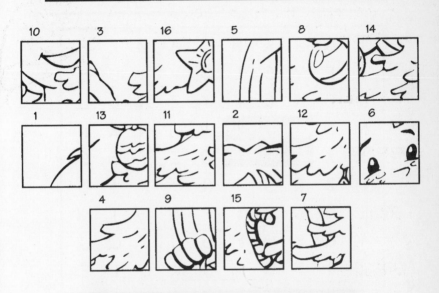

FIND THE FOUR

COMPLETE THE PUZZLE BELOW BY CROSSING OUT EVERY LETTER THAT APPEARS AT LEAST FOUR TIMES. USE THE REMAINING LETTERS TO COMPLETE THE SENTENCE.

```
F  Q  J  K  N  U  A  M  F  P
P  E  V  S  L  G  V  L  U  H
I  S  N  B  F  Y  Z  W  D  U
M  G  ▆▆▆▆▆  W  H  N  X  K
K  X  ▆▆▆▆▆  O  Z  Y  S  G
H  Z  R  J  I  Q  Y  X  I  B
L  B  W  Z  Y  P  W  F  T  M
V  N  X  S  H  U  C  V  Q  J
Q  I  P  B  M  J  K  G  L  E
```

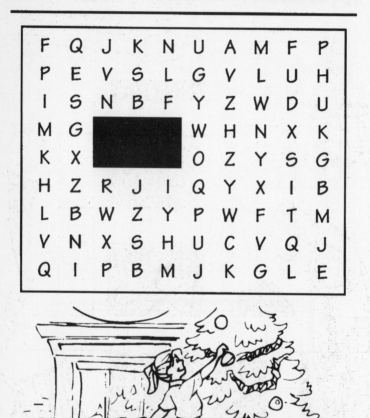

THE KIDS WERE OLD ENOUGH THIS YEAR TO

___ ___ ___ ___ ___ ___ ___ ___ THE TREE THEMSELVES.

86

PICTURE CLUES

THE PICTURES ARE YOUR ONLY CLUES TO COMPLETING THIS
CROSSWORD. THIS IS A BIT OF A BRAIN TEASER.

CAN YOU PICTURE IT?

THE PICTURES ARE YOUR CLUES. USE THE CIRCLED LETTERS TO
COMPLETE THE PUZZLE BELOW.

LOOK ◯◯◯◯◯◯◯
TO SEE WHAT JOY YOUR PRESENTS BRING.

DON'T LEAVE IT SCRAMBLED!

UNSCRAMBLE EACH WORD, THEN USE THE CIRCLED LETTERS TO COMPLETE THE PUZZLE BELOW . . . AND I HOPE IT DOESN'T HURT YOUR EYES!

"RLYOG OT DGO NI HET SGEHITH, NAD

" _____ __ ___ __ ___O_____, ___

NO ATREH CEEPA OT ENM NO OWMH

__ _____ ___O_O_ ___ __ ____

ISH VOAFR TRSES."

_O_ _____ _O_O_"

AWESOME!!

LUKE 2:14

THE GREATEST GIFT?

◯ ◯ ◯ ◯ ◯ ◯

PICTURE MAKER

YOU MAKE THE PICTURE. DRAW THE IMAGE FROM EACH FRAME AT THE TOP IN THE FRAME BELOW WITH THE MATCHING NUMBER.

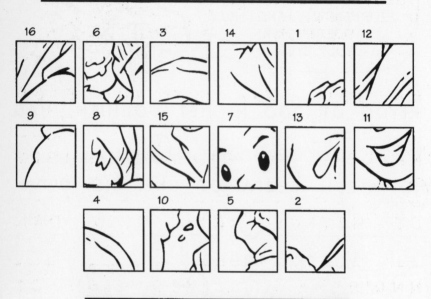

DON'T LEAVE IT SCRAMBLED!

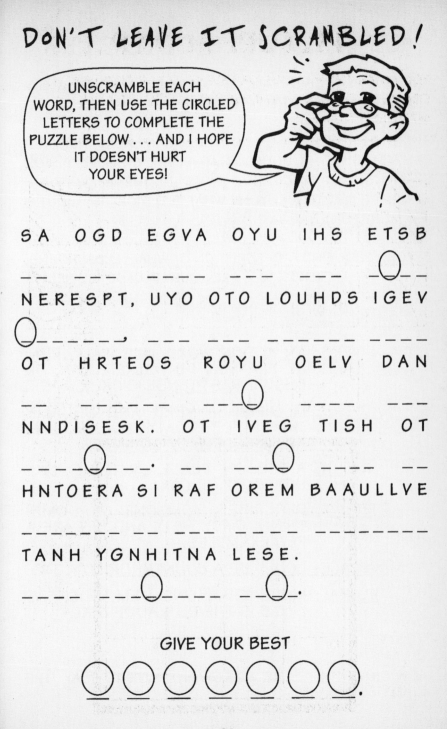

UNSCRAMBLE EACH WORD, THEN USE THE CIRCLED LETTERS TO COMPLETE THE PUZZLE BELOW . . . AND I HOPE IT DOESN'T HURT YOUR EYES!

SA   OGD   EGVA   OYU   IHS   ETSB

__ ___ ____ ___ ___ __(O)__

NERESPT, UYO OTO LOUHDS IGEV

(O)_____, ___ ___ _____ ____

OT   HRTEOS   ROYU   OELV   DAN

__ _____ __(O)_ ____ ___

NNDISESK. OT IVEG TISH OT

___(O)___. __ __(O)_ ____ __

HNTOERA SI RAF OREM BAAULLVE

_____ __ ___ ____ _____

TANH YGNHITNA LESE.

____ __(O)____ __(O)_.

GIVE YOUR BEST

(O) (O) (O) (O) (O) (O) (O) .

REALLY SILLY STORIES

YOU CAN PLAY THIS GAME BY YOURSELF, BUT IT'S A LOT MORE FUN TO PLAY WITH OTHERS.

ASK EACH PLAYER TO CALL OUT THE KIND OF WORD INDICATED IN EACH SPACE—A NOUN OR ADJECTIVE OR ADVERB, FOR EXAMPLE—AND PLACE THAT WORD IN THE APPROPRIATE SPACE. DO NOT TELL ANYONE WHAT THE STORY IS ABOUT—IT'S MORE FUN THAT WAY!

BELOW YOU'LL FIND A DESCRIPTION OF WHAT VERBS, NOUNS, ADJECTIVES, ADVERBS, ETC., ARE—JUST IN CASE YOU NEED A LITTLE HELP.

<u>VERB:</u> AN ACTION WORD, LIKE *WALK, RUN,* OR *FLY.* MAY BE *WALKED, RAN,* OR *FLEW,* IF <u>PAST TENSE</u> IS CALLED FOR.

<u>ADVERB:</u> MODIFIES A VERB AND USUALLY ENDS IN "LY." *SLOWLY* AND *CAREFULLY* ARE A COUPLE OF EXAMPLES.

<u>NOUN:</u> A PERSON, PLACE, OR THING, LIKE *BOY, BOAT,* OR *CAR.*

<u>ADJECTIVE:</u> DESCRIBES SOMEONE OR SOMETHING. *DIRTY, SILLY,* AND *BIG* ARE A FEW EXAMPLES.

<u>PLACE:</u> COULD BE A *COUNTRY* OR *CITY,* ETC.

<u>PLURAL:</u> MORE THAN ONE ITEM, SUCH AS *GIRLS* IS THE PLURAL OF *GIRL.*

NOW MOVE ON TO THE FOLLOWING PAGE TO PLAY THIS REALLY SILLY GAME!

REALLY SILLY STORIES

DON'T LOOK AT THE STORY BELOW. INSTEAD, FILL IN THE BLANKS IN THE LIST BELOW WITH THE REQUIRED WORDS. THEN FILL IN THE BLANKS IN THE STORY AND GET READY TO LAUGH UNCONTROLLABLY!

TIME OF DAY _____   PLURAL NOUN _____
NOUN _____   NOUN _____
NOUN _____   VERB _____
PLURAL NOUN _____   PLURAL NOUN _____
NOUN _____   VERB _____
NOUN _____   VERB ENDING IN "ING"
NOUN _____   _____
PLURAL NOUN _____   NAME OF SEASON
PLURAL NOUN _____   _____
ADJECTIVE _____   PLURAL NOUN _____
VERB ENDING IN "ING"   VERB ENDING IN "ING"
_____   _____
PLURAL NOUN _____   VERB ENDING IN "ING"
                                   _____

CHRISTMAS _____ HAD FINALLY ARRIVED AND THE
    TIME OF DAY

_____ WAS IN THE _____ OF UNWRAPPING THE
  NOUN   NOUN

_____ UNDER THE _____. THERE WAS A
  PLURAL NOUN   NOUN

LOT OF _____ BEING TOGETHER AND MUCH _____
    NOUN   NOUN

AS THEY EXCHANGED _____. THE _____ WERE
         PLURAL NOUN   PLURAL NOUN

PLEASED AS THEY NOTICED THEIR KIDS SEEMING TO BE

MORE _____ ABOUT THE _____ OF THE _____
    ADJECTIVE   VERB—"ING"   PLURAL NOUN

RATHER THAN THE RECEIVING OF _____. IT LOOKED LIKE
               PLURAL NOUN

THEY HAD MORE _____ WATCHING EACH OTHER _____
       NOUN   VERB

THE _____ THEY HAD CHOSEN FOR EACH OTHER, AND
  PLURAL NOUN

THIS WAS GOOD TO _____. THEY WERE _____ THE
        VERB   VERB—"ING"

TRUTH OF _____ IN THEIR _____. IT WASN'T
    NAME OF SEASON   PLURAL NOUN

ABOUT _____, IT WAS ABOUT _____.
  VERB—"ING"   VERB—"ING"

93

WHERE ARE THOSE VOWELS?

YOU'RE GOING TO HAVE TO CONCENTRATE FOR THIS ONE! VOWELS ARE HIDDEN IN THE PICTURE BELOW. YOU WILL NEED THEM TO COMPLETE THE PUZZLE.

"B__T THE ANG__L SA__D TO TH__M, 'DO NOT B__ AFRA__D. __ BRING YOU GOOD N__WS OF GR__AT JOY THAT W__LL B__ FOR ALL TH__ P__OPL__. TODAY __N TH__ TOWN OF DAV__D A SAV__OR HAS B__ __N BORN TO YO__; H__ __S CHR__ST TH__ LORD.'"

LUKE 2:10–11

94

JUST A REGULAR OLD CROSSWORD!

ACROSS
1. MOM'S MOM
2. INSIDE A TURKEY
3. OLD STYLE CUP
4. BED FOR JESUS
5. NOT A LONG BREAD

DOWN
1. IN A CHURCH STEEPLE
2. DOWNHILL VEHICLE
3. EASTERN KING
4. TO MOVE ALONG
5. GROUP OF MUSICIANS

FIND THE FOUR

COMPLETE THE PUZZLE BELOW BY CROSSING OUT EVERY LETTER THAT APPEARS AT LEAST FOUR TIMES. USE THE REMAINING LETTERS TO COMPLETE THE SENTENCE.

I'LL HAVE THAT BABY *COOKED* IN NO TIME!

C	N	R	L	K	E	P	H	C	F
G	I	O	V	D	U	Q	B	S	J
T	P	H	W	J	F	N	T	M	G
A	D	T	E	S	R	O	█	U	W
S	█	K	U	B	G	█	E	V	C
J	R	W	C	O	V	D	P	I	N
O	M	F	V	I	W	R	U	L	Q
E	Q	T	H	P	K	Q	M	S	H
K	B	I	M	D	G	N	B	F	J

MOM'S GOT A BUSY DAY AHEAD, AND RATHER THAN PLAY WITH THEIR NEW TOYS __ __ __ DAY, THE KIDS ARE HELPING TO PREPARE CHRISTMAS DINNER.

it's a MYSTERY

THIS IS A GREAT GAME TO PLAY AS YOU TRAVEL. YOU'LL NEED SOMEONE TO PLAY IT WITH, THOUGH, LIKE YOUR BROTHER OR SISTER OR FRIENDS.

BELOW IS A LIST OF PHRASES THAT NEED TO BE COMPLETED. SHOW THIS PUZZLE TO EACH PLAYER, WHO PICKS A LETTER TO FILL IN THE BLANKS, AND THEN HAS TEN SECONDS TO GUESS THE PHRASE. MOVE ON TO EACH PLAYER UNTIL THE MYSTERY IS SOLVED! AS THE HOST OF THIS GAME, YOU GET TO CHECK OUT THE SOLUTION FROM THE ANSWER PAGES AT THE BACK (IF YOU NEED TO)!

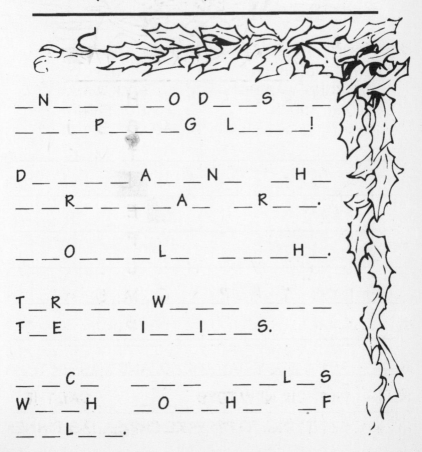

_ N _ _ _ _ _ O D _ _ S _ _ _
_ _ _ _ P _ _ _ G L _ _ _ _ !

D _ _ _ _ _ A _ _ N _ _ H _
_ _ R _ _ _ _ _ A _ _ R _ _ .

_ _ O _ _ L _ _ _ _ _ H _ _ .

T _ R _ _ _ W _ _ _ _ _ _ _ _
T _ E _ _ I _ _ I _ _ S .

_ _ C _ _ _ _ _ _ _ _ L _ S
W _ _ H _ O _ _ H _ _ F
_ _ L _ _ .

TRAVELLIN' RHYMES

THIS IS A GREAT GAME TO PLAY AS YOU TRAVEL. YOU'LL NEED SOMEONE TO PLAY IT WITH, THOUGH, LIKE YOUR BROTHER OR SISTER OR FRIENDS.

BELOW IS A LIST OF WORD PAIRS THAT RHYME WITH EACH OTHER. YOUR JOB IS TO CALL OUT THE WORDS AND HAVE THE PLAYERS COME UP WITH THE SILLIEST RHYMES. WRITE THE BEST ON THE SPACES BELOW.

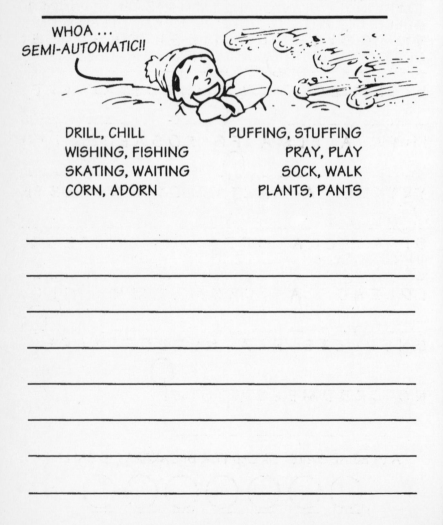

WHOA ... SEMI-AUTOMATIC!!

DRILL, CHILL	PUFFING, STUFFING
WISHING, FISHING	PRAY, PLAY
SKATING, WAITING	SOCK, WALK
CORN, ADORN	PLANTS, PANTS

DON'T LEAVE IT SCRAMBLED!

UNSCRAMBLE EACH WORD, THEN USE THE CIRCLED LETTERS TO COMPLETE THE PUZZLE BELOW . . . AND I HOPE IT DOESN'T HURT YOUR EYES!

NI   GBLEUMI,   MRSITSAHC   SI

__ _____, _____ __

BTELDAECRE NO TMHRSSIAC VEE,

_____ _____ ___,

IHTW A ELMA FO FOSAEDO NAD

____ _ _____ __ _____ ___

YRTKUE. A NARTADLOTII RSDESTE

_____. _ _____ _____

SI A ECKA MDEA IHWT MCEAR,

__ _ ____ ____ ____ _____,

LDLEAC   A   CRSMATISH   GLO.

_____ _ _____ ___.

SNSPRETE REA NEPDOE YAREL,

_____ ___ _____ _____,

NO CRBDMEEE TXSIH!

__ _____ ____!

A SPECIAL SWEET BREAD FOR BREAKFAST IS CALLED

◯ ◯ ◯ ◯ ◯ ◯ ◯.

PICTURE MAKER

YOU MAKE THE PICTURE. DRAW THE IMAGE FROM EACH
FRAME AT THE TOP IN THE FRAME BELOW WITH THE
MATCHING NUMBER.

UP OR DOWN?

UNSCRAMBLE THE WORDS, THEN IT'S UP TO YOU TO FIND WHERE EACH WORD GOES. WE PUT A FEW LETTERS IN TO HELP.

LCOSHANI _____   UCEL _____

EUMIGLB _____   ESSTRDE _____

PRFIEECLA _____   RWCNO _____

GCKNITSOS _____   ETFAHR _____

MEDEER _____   EGTA _____

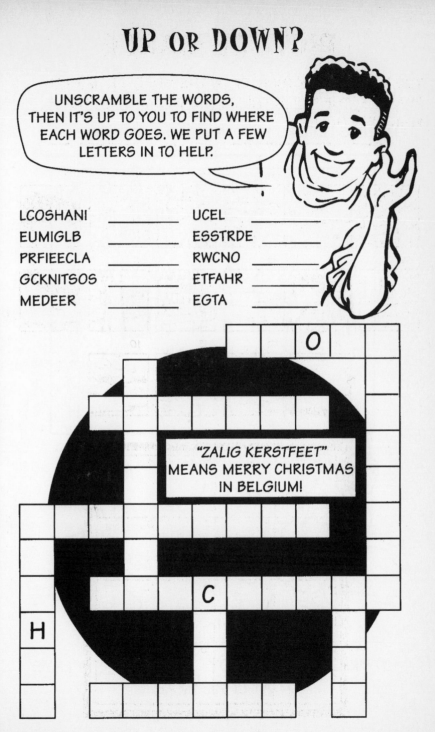

"ZALIG KERSTFEET" MEANS MERRY CHRISTMAS IN BELGIUM!

FIND THE FOUR

COMPLETE THE PUZZLE BELOW BY CROSSING OUT EVERY LETTER THAT APPEARS AT LEAST FOUR TIMES. USE THE REMAINING LETTERS TO COMPLETE THE SENTENCE.

D	N	J	C	H	T	A	Q	G	K
G	B	S	P	E	V	U	J	M	R
Q	U	O	M	W	X	I	V	D	S
C	H	V	R	A	Y	C	Y	G	A
I	P	G	T	D	X	W		Q	I
N	E	W	M	S	H	B		U	P
L	S	Y	B	N	V	X	Y	X	E
R	I	U	J	Q	F	W	T	B	M
J	A	P	T	C	E	R	D	N	H

THAT'S SOME COSTUME.

YOU'RE ONE TA' TALK ...!

IN BRAZIL, THEY ENJOY __ __ __ __ PLAYS AT CHRISTMAS.

CAN YOU FIND THE WORDS?

ALL THESE
WORDS ARE HIDDEN IN
THE PUZZLE BELOW.
HAVE FUN!

FESTIVAL
PAGEANT
SINGING
ORCHIDS
CUSTOMS

DANCING
PLAYS
FANDANGO
ORNAMENTS
DANCE

```
K C Q S B R       L B F J L
J Y P A G E A N T P Q P H T
S N D N H F E S T I V A L
  I A F O R N A M E N T S
  F N K A J D N C W D G
  P C G S N M B V T V O N
  L I C I K D W N Q E R C P
P A N Q H N R A H C G C K
G Y G L F V G T N V L H F
B S N M N E P A K G R I
P D R V A T D J L S O D N
  T W Q C U S T O M S R
  J C W L     M D T Y W
  G S H           F M B X
```

LET'S MAZE AROUND

TRAVEL THROUGH SOUTH AMERICA TO GET TO BRAZIL.

ALL JUMBLED UP

HEY . . . THIS ONE WILL BE FUN!
FIND THE OPPOSITE OF EACH WORD,
THEN USE THE CIRCLED LETTERS TO
COMPLETE THE PUZZLE BELOW.

MERRY ◯ _ _

DINNER _ _ ◯ _ _ ◯ _ _

SOUTH ◯◯ _ _ _

RECORDED _ _ ◯ _

STRAIGHT _ _ _ - ◯ _ _

SLEEP ◯ _ _ _ _

RUN _ ◯ _

IN BRAZIL, "B ◯◯ S F ◯ STA ◯

E ◯ E ◯ I ◯ ANO ◯ O ◯ O ,"

MEANS HAPPY HOLIDAYS.

WHERE ARE THOSE VOWELS?

YOU'RE GOING TO HAVE TO CONCENTRATE FOR THIS ONE! VOWELS ARE HIDDEN IN THE PICTURE BELOW. YOU WILL NEED THEM TO COMPLETE THE PUZZLE.

B _ X _ NG D _ Y _ S THE B _ G
CHR _ STM _ S CELEBR _ T _ _ N
_ N ENGL _ ND _ ND _ S _
N _ T _ _ N _ L H _ L _ D _ Y. B _ XED
PRESENTS, PL _ CED _ N CHURCHES
THR _ UGH _ UT THE YE _ R, _ RE
_ PENED _ N TH _ S D _ Y.

LESS SHALL BE FIRST

PLACE THE WORDS BELOW INTO THE PUZZLE ACCORDING TO THE NUMBER OF LETTERS IN EACH WORD, BEGINNING WITH THE WORD THAT HAS THE FEWEST LETTERS. THEN, UNSCRAMBLE THE CIRCLED LETTERS TO COMPLETE THE ANSWER BELOW.

HOLIDAY   NATIONAL
PRINCIPLE   ACTS
BOXED   STONED
LED

OUCH!

THIS DAY IS ALSO CALLED

SAINT ○ ○ ○ ○ ○ ○ ○ DAY, AFTER THE CHRISTIAN MARTYR WHO WAS STONED TO DEATH, AS TOLD IN THE BOOK OF ACTS.

TRAVELLIN' RHYMES

THIS IS A GREAT GAME TO PLAY AS YOU TRAVEL. YOU'LL NEED SOMEONE TO PLAY IT WITH, THOUGH, LIKE YOUR BROTHER OR SISTER OR FRIENDS.

BELOW IS A LIST OF WORD PAIRS THAT RHYME WITH EACH OTHER. YOUR JOB IS TO CALL OUT THE WORDS AND HAVE THE PLAYERS COME UP WITH THE SILLIEST RHYMES. WRITE THE BEST ON THE SPACES BELOW.

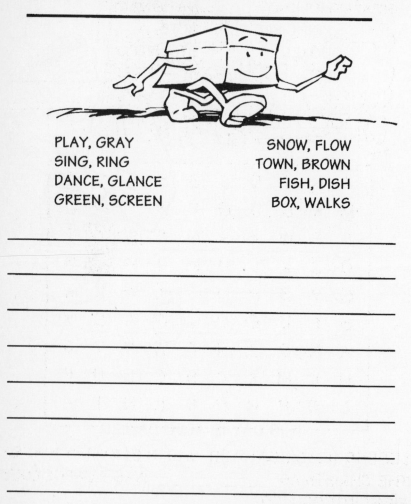

PLAY, GRAY
SING, RING
DANCE, GLANCE
GREEN, SCREEN

SNOW, FLOW
TOWN, BROWN
FISH, DISH
BOX, WALKS

_____

_____

_____

_____

_____

_____

_____

FIND THE FOUR

COMPLETE THE PUZZLE BELOW BY CROSSING OUT EVERY LETTER THAT APPEARS AT LEAST FOUR TIMES. USE THE REMAINING LETTERS TO COMPLETE THE SENTENCE.

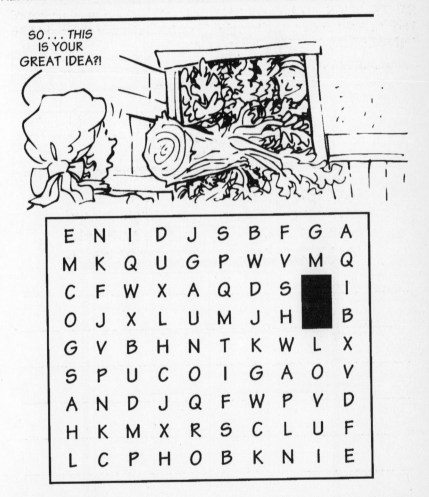

SO . . . THIS IS YOUR GREAT IDEA?!

E	N	I	D	J	S	B	F	G	A
M	K	Q	U	G	P	W	V	M	Q
C	F	W	X	A	Q	D	S		I
O	J	X	L	U	M	J	H		B
G	V	B	H	N	T	K	W	L	X
S	P	U	C	O	I	G	A	O	V
A	N	D	J	Q	F	W	P	V	D
H	K	M	X	R	S	C	L	U	F
L	C	P	H	O	B	K	N	I	E

LEGEND TELLS US THAT IT WAS IN GERMANY WHERE THE CHRISTMAS __ __ __ __ WAS SUPPOSEDLY FIRST INTRODUCED.

PICTURE MAKER

YOU MAKE THE PICTURE. DRAW THE IMAGE FROM EACH FRAME AT THE TOP IN THE FRAME BELOW WITH THE MATCHING NUMBER.

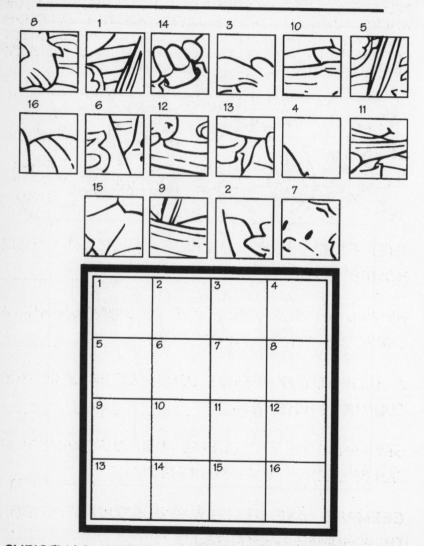

CHRISTMAS BEGINS EARLY IN GERMANY WITH THE ANNUAL TOY FAIR, OR "CHRISTKINDLESMARKT."

WHO, WHAT, WHERE

THIS IS A GREAT GAME TO PLAY AS YOU TRAVEL. YOU'LL NEED SOMEONE TO PLAY IT WITH, THOUGH, LIKE YOUR BROTHER OR SISTER OR FRIENDS.

BELOW IS A LIST OF QUESTIONS THAT NEED A "WHO, WHAT, OR WHERE" ANSWER. EACH PLAYER HAS TEN SECONDS TO ANSWER. AS THE HOST OF THIS GAME, YOU GET TO CHECK OUT THE SOLUTION FROM THE ANSWER PAGES AT THE BACK (IF YOU NEED TO)!

THEY FIRST BEGAN TO BRING THESE INTO THEIR HOMES. *WHAT* IS IT? _____

HE WAS THE ONE BEHIND THE REFORMATION AND A CHRISTMAS SYMBOL . *WHO* IS HE? _____

A HUGE TOY FAIR KICKS OFF CHRISTMAS IN THIS COUNTRY. *WHERE* IS IT? _____

GERMANS LOVE TO DECORATE AROUND A FRAME THAT CAN BE SEEN OUTSIDE. *WHAT* IS IT? _____

GERMANS LOVE TO HEAR THIS GROUP WHO VISIT THEIR HOMES. *WHO* ARE THEY? _____

it's a MYSTERY

THIS IS A GREAT GAME TO PLAY AS YOU TRAVEL. YOU'LL NEED SOMEONE TO PLAY IT WITH, THOUGH, LIKE YOUR BROTHER OR SISTER OR FRIENDS.

BELOW IS A LIST OF PHRASES THAT NEED TO BE COMPLETED. SHOW THIS PUZZLE TO EACH PLAYER, WHO PICKS A LETTER TO FILL IN THE BLANKS, AND THEN HAS TEN SECONDS TO GUESS THE PHRASE. MOVE ON TO EACH PLAYER UNTIL THE MYSTERY IS SOLVED! AS THE HOST OF THIS GAME, YOU GET TO CHECK OUT THE SOLUTION FROM THE ANSWER PAGES AT THE BACK (IF YOU NEED TO)!

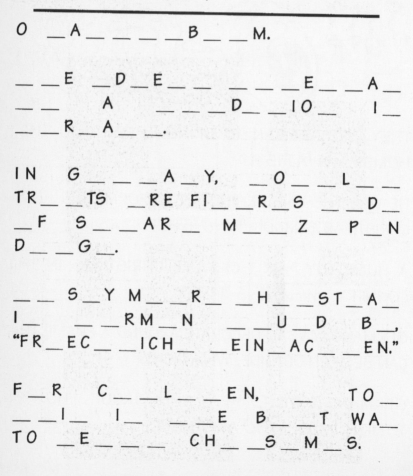

O __ A __ __ __ __ __ B __ __ M.

__ __ E __ D E __ __ __ __ __ E __ __ A __
__ __   A   __ __ __ D __ __ IO __   I __
__ __ R __ A __ __.

IN   G __ __ __ A __ Y,   __ O __ __ L __ __
TR __ __ TS   __ RE FI __ __ R __ S   __ __ D __
__ F S __ __ AR __ M __ __ Z __ P __ N
D __ __ G __.

__ __   S __ Y M __ __ R __ __ H __ __ ST __ A __
I __   __ __ RM __ N   __ __ U __ D B __,
"FR __ EC __ __ ICH __ __ EIN __ AC __ __ EN."

F __ R   C __ __ L __ __ EN,   __   TO __
__ __ I __ I __ __ __ E B __ __ T WA __
TO __ E __ __ __ CH __ __ S __ M __ S.

112

JUST A REGULAR OLD CROSSWORD!

ACROSS

1. FUN CELEBRATION
2. SEASONAL EVENT
3. A PERFORMANCE
4. COLOR OF RIBBON
5. BRINGS LIGHT

DOWN

1. SWEDISH PROCESSIONS
2. COUNTRY OF BLONDS
3. DECORATIVE LIGHT
4. DRESSLIKE GARMENT
5. VERY SHORT IN DECEMBER

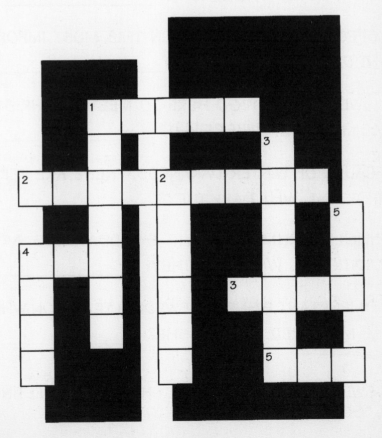

WHO, WHAT, WHERE

THIS IS A GREAT GAME TO PLAY AS YOU TRAVEL. YOU'LL NEED SOMEONE TO PLAY IT WITH, THOUGH, LIKE YOUR BROTHER OR SISTER OR FRIENDS.

BELOW IS A LIST OF QUESTIONS THAT NEED A "WHO, WHAT, OR WHERE" ANSWER. EACH PLAYER HAS TEN SECONDS TO ANSWER. AS THE HOST OF THIS GAME, YOU GET TO CHECK OUT THE SOLUTION FROM THE ANSWER PAGES AT THE BACK (IF YOU NEED TO)!

———————————————

IN THIS COUNTRY, THE SHORTEST, DARKEST DAY IS DECEMBER 22. *WHERE* IS IT? _____

A SPECIAL MEAL IS EATEN ON THIS MOST IMPORTANT DAY. *WHAT* DAY IS IT? _____

IN SWEDEN, MANY *GO* HERE TO MEET ON CHRISTMAS MORNING. *WHERE* IS IT? _____

BECAUSE OF WINTER DARKNESS, THESE ARE VERY IMPORTANT. *WHAT* ARE THEY? _____

KRINGLE, KRUMKAKE, AND SANDBAKKELS ARE TRADITIONAL. *WHAT* ARE THEY? _____

AN IMPORTANT FIGURE IN SWEDISH TRADITION WHO WAS MARTYRED. *WHO* IS SHE? _____

IN SWEDEN, THE TRADITIONAL CHRISTMAS GREETING IS, "GOD JUL."

PICTURE MAKER

YOU MAKE THE PICTURE. DRAW THE IMAGE FROM EACH FRAME AT THE TOP IN THE FRAME BELOW WITH THE MATCHING NUMBER.

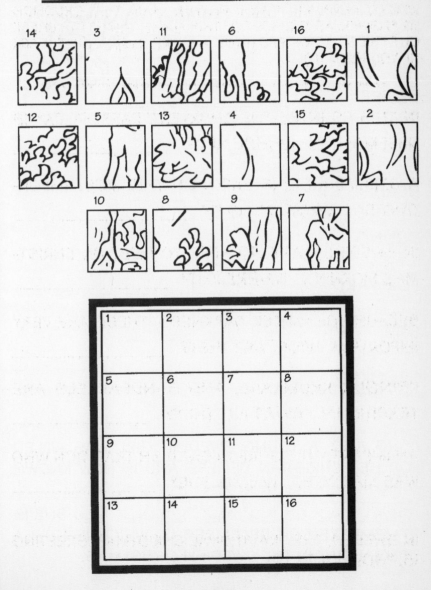

ALL JUMBLED UP

HEY . . . THIS ONE WILL BE FUN!
FIND THE OPPOSITE OF EACH WORD,
THEN USE THE CIRCLED LETTERS TO
COMPLETE THE PUZZLE BELOW.

BELIEF   _ _ (_) _

NIGHT   _ (_) _

BLACK   _ _ (_) _ _

YOUNG   _ (_) _

FORWARD   _ _ (_) _ _ _ _ _

SIT   _ (_) _ _ _

CROOKED   (_) _ _ _ _ _ _

LONG AGO, A YOUNG SWEDISH GIRL WAS KILLED
FOR HER CHRISTIAN BELIEFS AND IS NOW KNOWN

AS (_)(_). (_)(_)(_)(_)(_). SHE IS
REMEMBERED ON DECEMBER 13, WHICH IS NOW A
SPECIAL DAY IN THE SWEDISH CHRISTMAS.

CAN YOU FIND THE WORDS?

ALL THESE
WORDS ARE HIDDEN IN
THE PUZZLE BELOW.
HAVE FUN!

ST. LUCIA
CROWN
SWEDEN
GINGERBREAD
LIGHT
BREAD

HOLIDAY
DRESS
BEADS
ROBE
RIBBON
GARLAND

```
        B L E J
      D G B F L N
      K O L G Q P
      R H P I M K
F C R I B B O N G D R E S S
H S R H M P G G D H F J M G
C K T . O J C M E N B T P B L
      L W F N R H Q N
      I U N B B J E K
      I D L C K R D L B I
      D A H G I E E D E H
      G Y B J W A C A A K
      T C D S E D H F D H
    G A R L A N D B G S C W
```

LETTER CLUES

TO DECODE THIS MESSAGE, YOU'LL NEED TO TAKE THE LETTER FROM EACH NUMBERED CLUE AND MATCH IT TO THE NUMBERED SPACE IN THE PUZZLE BELOW.

---

1. THIS LETTER IS FOUND IN BOTH *DRESS* AND *GET*.

   _____

2. IT'S FOUND ONCE IN *ROBE* AND TWICE IN *RIBBON*.

   _____

3. FOUND FIRST IN BOTH *CANDLES* AND IN *CANDY*.

   _____

4. FOUND FIRST IN BOTH *FRANCE* AND IN *FRENCH*.

   _____

5. THIS LETTER BEGINS *X-RAY* AND ENDS *BOX*.

   _____

6. THIS LETTER IS FOUND IN *REST* BUT NOT IN *BEST*.

   _____

IN __ __ AN __ __, __H __ ISTMAS T __ __ __ S
    4 6   3 1   3 6   6 1 1

A __ __ D __ __ O __ AT __ D WITH WHIT __
  6 1   1 3 6   1   1

__ ANDL __ S AND __ __ D __ I __ __ ONS. __ V __ N
3   1   6 1 6 2 2   1 1

T __ __ __ S OUTSID __ A __ __ D __ __ O __ AT __ D
 6 1 1   1   6 1   1 3 6 1

AND LIT TH __ OUGH TH __ NIGHT. IN TH __
          6   1   1

LANGUAG __ OF TH __ __ __ __ N __ H, ON __
       1   1 4 6 1 3   1

WOULD H __ A __ M __ __ __ Y __ H __ ISTMAS AS,
        1 6   1 6 6   3 6

"JOY __ U __ NO __ L."
     1   5   1

LESS SHALL BE FIRST

PLACE THE WORDS BELOW INTO THE PUZZLE ACCORDING TO THE NUMBER OF LETTERS IN EACH WORD, BEGINNING WITH THE WORD THAT HAS THE FEWEST LETTERS. THEN, UNSCRAMBLE THE CIRCLED LETTERS TO COMPLETE THE ANSWER BELOW.

HOLIDAY   BOW
ROBE   BEAUTIFUL
PICTURES   WINDOW
BREAD

CANDLES AND ◯ ◯ ◯ ◯ ◯ ◯ ◯

ARE A PART OF A FRENCH CHRISTMAS.

DON'T LEAVE IT SCRAMBLED!

UNSCRAMBLE EACH WORD, THEN USE THE CIRCLED LETTERS TO COMPLETE THE PUZZLE BELOW . . . AND I HOPE IT DOESN'T HURT YOUR EYES!

OESTH NI NADII HOW EAR FO

_ _ _ _ _   _ _   _ _ _ _ _   _ _ _   _ _ _   _ _

HET THRNSIAIC TAHIF TECLERBAE

_ _ _   _ _ _ _ _ _ _ _   _ _ _ _ _   _ _ _ _ _ _ _ _

AITHMSSCR SA LELW. TYEH

_ _ _ _ _ _ _ _ _   _ _   _ _ _ _ .   _ _ _ _

OTREDECA HREIT HHCRUSCE IHWT

_ _ _ _ _ _ _ _   _ _ _ _ _   _ _ _ _ _ _ _ _   _ _ _ _

A TBFLUEUIA WLFEOR ELALCD

_   _ _ _ _ _ _ _ _   _ _ _ _ _   _ _ _ _ _ _

HTE EITAPOSTIN NAD AGONM RO

_ _ _   _ _ _ _ _ _ _ _ _   _ _ _   _ _ _ _ _   _ _

BNAANA ESRET RAE LLUFOYLRCO

_ _ _ _ _ _   _ _ _ _ _   _ _ _   _ _ _ _ _ _ _ _ _ _

RTDNONEMEA.

_ _ _ _ _ _ _ _ _ _ .

IN INDIA, ◯◯◯◯◯◯ IS CALLED, "BAKSHEESH."

LET'S MAZE AROUND

SOME CHRISTIANS IN INDIA DECORATE THEIR HOMES WITH SMALL CLAY LAMPS. MAKE YOUR WAY THROUGH THE STREETS TO GET HOME IN TIME FOR THE CELEBRATION.

UP OR DOWN?

UNSCRAMBLE THE WORDS, THEN IT'S UP TO YOU TO FIND WHERE EACH WORD GOES. WE PUT A FEW LETTERS IN TO HELP.

FPTOORO _____   OYJ _____
TSNPEOAIIT _____ DNAII _____
IASTELFV _____   ISFTG _____
NHDGTIMI _____   SAMS _____
YRHACTI _____   WLLA _____
MIYFLA _____   TPO _____

122

WHERE ARE THOSE VOWELS?

YOU'RE GOING TO HAVE TO CONCENTRATE FOR THIS ONE! VOWELS ARE HIDDEN IN THE PICTURE BELOW. YOU WILL NEED THEM TO COMPLETE THE PUZZLE.

IN FINL _ ND, CHRISTM _ S EVE, CHRISTM _ S D _ Y, _ ND B _ XING D _ Y _ RE HELD T _ BE THE THREE H _ LY D _ YS. CHRISTM _ S DINNER IS C _ NSIDERED _ FE _ ST _ FTER _ LIGHT BRE _ KF _ ST _ F PL _ M J _ ICE _ ND RICE P _ RRIDGE.

PICTURE CLUES

THE PICTURES ARE YOUR ONLY CLUES TO COMPLETING THIS
CROSSWORD. THIS IS A BIT OF A BRAIN TEASER.

COMPLETE THE PUZZLE BELOW BY CROSSING OUT EVERY LETTER THAT APPEARS AT LEAST FOUR TIMES. USE THE REMAINING LETTERS TO COMPLETE THE SENTENCE.

I CAN'T *READ* IT . . . MUCH LESS SAY IT!

```
D Q I F C V J M Q A
N L U G P D X B Y V
K B V E M Y W Z T J
S R Y K J A Z F G M
G N C Z        C D X
P W L D N Z H U P W
E U X F Y E L X K F
M A S U O G A V B Q
J Q B W N K P E L C
```

THE CHRISTMAS GREETING IN RUSSIA IS

"_ _ _ _ _ _ _ RAZDAJETSJA."

It's a Mystery

THIS IS A GREAT GAME TO PLAY AS YOU TRAVEL. YOU'LL NEED SOMEONE TO PLAY IT WITH, THOUGH, LIKE YOUR BROTHER OR SISTER OR FRIENDS.

BELOW IS A LIST OF PHRASES THAT NEED TO BE COMPLETED. SHOW THIS PUZZLE TO EACH PLAYER, WHO PICKS A LETTER TO FILL IN THE BLANKS, AND THEN HAS TEN SECONDS TO GUESS THE PHRASE. MOVE ON TO EACH PLAYER UNTIL THE MYSTERY IS SOLVED! AS THE HOST OF THIS GAME, YOU GET TO CHECK OUT THE SOLUTION FROM THE ANSWER PAGES AT THE BACK (IF YOU NEED TO)!

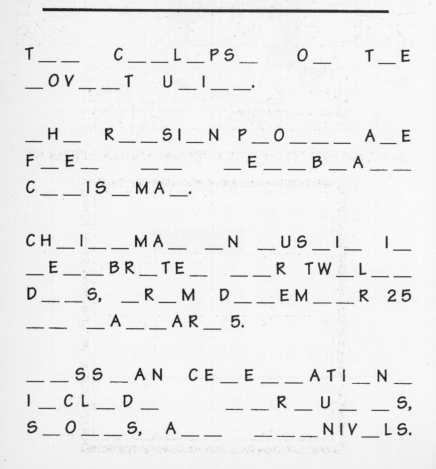

```
T _ _    C _ _ L _ PS _    O _    T _ E
_ O V _ _ T   U _ I _ _.


_ H _    R _ _ SI _ N   P _ O _ _ _    A _ E
F _ E _    _ _    _ E _ _ B _ A _ _ _
C _ _ IS _ MA _.


CH _ I _ _ MA _    _ N   _ US _ I _   I _
_ E _ _ BR _ TE _    _ _ R   TW _ L _ _ _
D _ _ S,   _ R _ M   D _ _ EM _ _ _ R  25
_ _    _ A _ _ AR _  5.


_ _ SS _ AN   CE _ E _ _ ATI _ N _
I _ CL _ D _ _    _ _ R _ U _ _ S,
S _ O _ _ S,   A _ _ _    _ _ _ NIV _ LS.
```

PICTURE MAKER

YOU MAKE THE PICTURE. DRAW THE IMAGE FROM EACH FRAME AT THE TOP IN THE FRAME BELOW WITH THE MATCHING NUMBER.

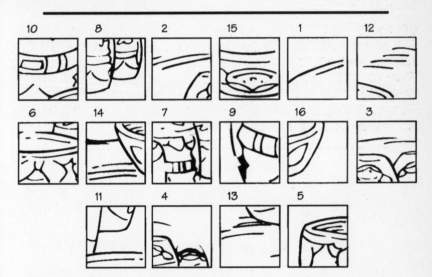

MATRYOSHKU DOLLS, A TRADITIONAL RUSSIAN PRESENT.

LETTER CLUES

TO DECODE THIS MESSAGE, YOU'LL NEED TO TAKE THE LETTER FROM EACH NUMBERED CLUE AND MATCH IT TO THE NUMBERED SPACE IN THE PUZZLE BELOW.

_____

1. THIS LETTER BEGINS BOTH *HEAR* AND *HERE*.

   _____

2. THIS LETTER ENDS BOTH *BLOCK* AND *BLACK*.

   _____

3. THIS LETTER IS FOUND IN *CAST* BUT NOT IN *LAST*.

   _____

4. IT ENDS THE WORD *CAT* AND BEGINS THE WORD *TOY*.

   _____

5. IT APPEARS TWICE IN *SOON* AND ONCE IN *HOT*.

   _____

6. IT'S FOUND ONCE IN *FIVE* AND TWICE IN *VALVE*.

   _____

7. THIS LETTER IS FOUND IN *GIFT* BUT NOT IN *RIFT*.

   _____

8. THIS LETTER BEGINS BOTH *BLOCK* AND *BLACK*.

   _____

```
_ _ R I S _ I A N S    I N    _ _ N _    _ _ N _
3 1     4               1 5 7  2 5 7

_ A _ E   A D A P _ E D    _ _ E    _ _ R I S _ M A S
1 6               4        4 1      3 1     4

_ E L E _ R A _ I _ N   I N _ _   A N   E A S _ E R N
3     8   4 5          4 5                    4

S E _ _ I N _ .   N A _ I _ I _ Y   S _ E N E S   A N D
    4 4   7       4 6 4             3

_ _ R I S _ M A S    _ A R D S    _ A _ E    A
3 1     4            3            1 6

_ _ I N E S E   L _ _ _    A N D   A R E   _ E R Y
3 1             5 5 2                      6

A R _ I S _ I _ .
    4     4 3
```

128

CAN YOU FIND THE WORDS?

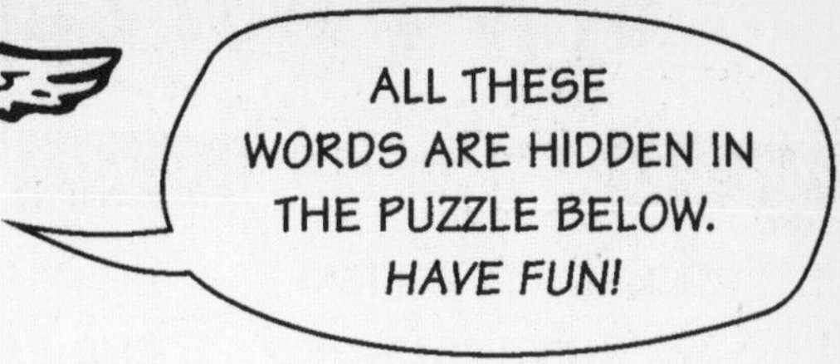

ALL THESE
WORDS ARE HIDDEN IN
THE PUZZLE BELOW.
HAVE FUN!

HONG   STREAMER
KONG   CARDS
CHINESE   LAMPS
EASTERN   NATIVITY

```
G P C L H O N G Y N
C T M S K O N G J R F
H V B W D S K Y
N I R F P Q T N
J D Q F N M Z L G A W J
H C S G K A E Y R S T B K
A Z L T P S B R I
V R J N W Q E M V
V B D T F D K H M A D I N G
L G P C Y T S A R S F T F P
F Q W H E M L T B Y S
B K R F N T E Z K V
Z L S T K Q D P R W B F C
C J M S R H V C F N H Y M K
```

JUST A REGULAR OLD CROSSWORD!

ACROSS

1. RETURNED TO CHINA
2. EASTERN LANGUAGE
3. PLACES OF WORSHIP

DOWN

1. CHINESE WORD PICTURE
2. CHINESE PAPER ORNAMENT
3. LONG PAPER DECORATION

130

PICTURE CLUES

THE PICTURES ARE YOUR ONLY CLUES TO COMPLETING THIS CROSSWORD. THIS IS A BIT OF A BRAIN TEASER.

ALL JUMBLED UP

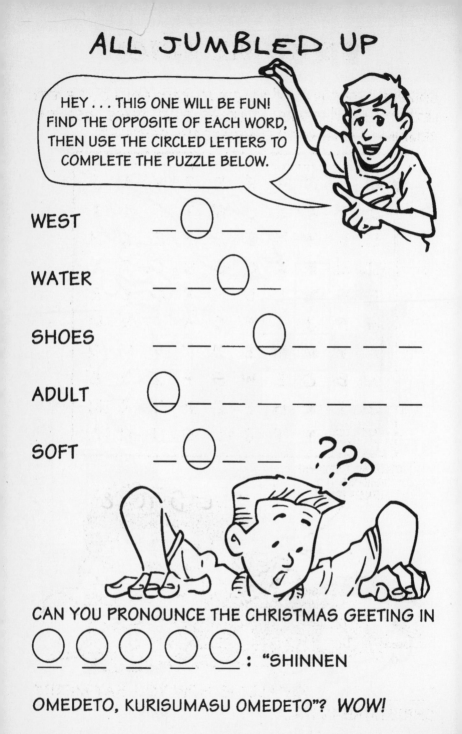

HEY . . . THIS ONE WILL BE FUN! FIND THE OPPOSITE OF EACH WORD, THEN USE THE CIRCLED LETTERS TO COMPLETE THE PUZZLE BELOW.

WEST _ _ Ⓞ _ _

WATER _ _ Ⓞ _

SHOES _ _ Ⓞ _ _ _ _

ADULT Ⓞ _ _ _ _ _ _

SOFT _ Ⓞ _ _

CAN YOU PRONOUNCE THE CHRISTMAS GEETING IN

◯ ◯ ◯ ◯ ◯ _ _ _ _ _ : "SHINNEN

OMEDETO, KURISUMASU OMEDETO"? *WOW!*

132

FIND THE FOUR

COMPLETE THE PUZZLE BELOW BY CROSSING OUT EVERY LETTER THAT APPEARS AT LEAST FOUR TIMES. USE THE REMAINING LETTERS TO COMPLETE THE SENTENCE.

D	R	W	A	R	K	Z	V	A	J
J	T	X	Z	J	W	T	P	I	X
L	D	V	Y	D	G	F	S	K	H
Q	M	F	X	Q	S	U	C	T	Y
E	S	W	L	C	H	R	G	E	R
H	P	J	I	P	Q	A	I	N	M
A	V	M	M	L	X	Y	V	M	Q
K	B	C	E	W	S	F	Z	D	S
G	I	K	H	E	Z	P	Y	R	M
F	G	Y	T	C	L	O	J	H	A

ITALIAN CUSTOMS? THEY'RE THE GREATEST!

"__ __ __ __ NATALE" IS HOW YOU SAY MERRY CHRISTMAS IN ITALY.

WHO, WHAT, WHERE

THIS IS A GREAT GAME TO PLAY AS YOU TRAVEL. YOU'LL NEED SOMEONE TO PLAY IT WITH, THOUGH, LIKE YOUR BROTHER OR SISTER OR FRIENDS.

BELOW IS A LIST OF QUESTIONS THAT NEED A "WHO, WHAT, OR WHERE" ANSWER. EACH PLAYER HAS TEN SECONDS TO ANSWER. AS THE HOST OF THIS GAME, YOU GET TO CHECK OUT THE SOLUTION FROM THE ANSWER PAGES AT THE BACK (IF YOU NEED TO)!

CHILDREN HOPE THAT "GESÚ BAMBINO" WILL BRING THEM GIFTS. *WHO* IS HE? _____

"PRESEPIO" IS AN ITALIAN NAME FOR A FAMILIAR CHRISTMAS SCENE. *WHAT* IS IT? _____

THESE ARE SPECIAL "BAGS" THAT MEN MAKE MUSIC ON. *WHAT* ARE THEY?

_____

IN ITALY, ONLY THIS MEAT IS EATEN ON THE FAST AT CHRISTMAS EVE. *WHAT* IS IT? _____

NO ITALIAN MEAL CAN BE COMPLETE WITHOUT THIS TRADITIONAL DISH. *WHAT* IS IT? _____

MUSICIANS DRESS IN SHEEPSKIN JACKETS AS A REMINDER OF THESE WHO WERE PRESENT AT CHRIST'S BIRTH. *WHO* ARE THEY? _____

LET'S MAZE AROUND

HELP THE MUSICIANS FIND THEIR WAY TO THE CHRISTMAS FEAST.

TRAVELLIN' RHYMES

THIS IS A GREAT GAME TO PLAY AS YOU TRAVEL. YOU'LL NEED SOMEONE TO PLAY IT WITH, THOUGH, LIKE YOUR BROTHER OR SISTER OR FRIENDS.

BELOW IS A LIST OF WORD PAIRS THAT RHYME WITH EACH OTHER. YOUR JOB IS TO CALL OUT THE WORDS AND HAVE THE PLAYERS COME UP WITH THE SILLIEST RHYMES. WRITE THE BEST ON THE SPACES BELOW.

FISH, DISH   HEAR, MIRROR
STREET, MEAT   FAST, PAST
JOY, TOY   DAY, PLAY
LIGHT, BRIGHT   EIGHT, ATE
JUICE, LOOSE   SPEED, FEED

DON'T LEAVE IT SCRAMBLED!

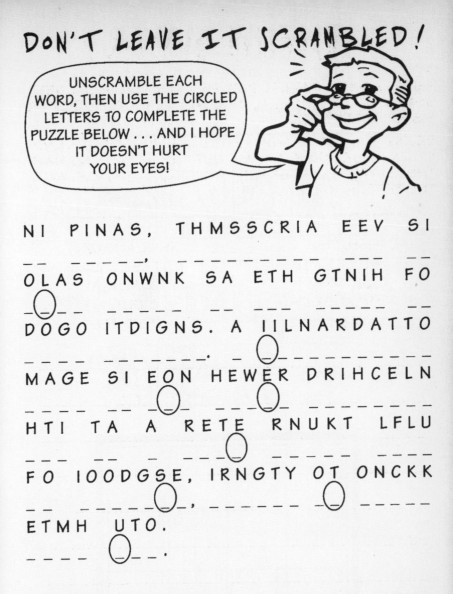

UNSCRAMBLE EACH WORD, THEN USE THE CIRCLED LETTERS TO COMPLETE THE PUZZLE BELOW... AND I HOPE IT DOESN'T HURT YOUR EYES!

NI PINAS, THMSSCRIA EEV SI

_ _ _ _ _ _ _ _ _, _ _ _ _ _ _ _ _ _ _ _ _ _ _ _

OLAS ONWNK SA ETH GTNIH FO

_ _ _ _ _ _ _ _ _ _ _ _ _ _ _ _ _ _ _ _

DOGO ITDIGNS. A IILNARDATTO

_ _ _ _ _ _ _ _ _ _ _. _ _ _ _ _ _ _ _ _ _ _

MAGE SI EON HEWER DRIHCELN

_ _ _ _ _ _ _ _ _ _ _ _ _ _ _ _ _ _ _

HTI TA A RETE RNUKT LFLU

_ _ _ _ _ _ _ _ _ _ _ _ _ _ _ _

FO IOODGSE, IRNGTY OT ONCKK

_ _ _ _ _ _ _ _ _, _ _ _ _ _ _ _ _

ETMH UTO.

_ _ _ _ _ _ _.

SPAIN HAS A LEGEND OF A COAL MINER, NAMED

◯ ◯ ◯ ◯ ◯ Z ◯ ◯ ◯ , WHO

CAME DOWN FROM A MOUNTAIN TO ANNOUNCE THE BIRTH OF CHRIST.

PICTURE MAKER

YOU MAKE THE PICTURE. DRAW THE IMAGE FROM EACH FRAME AT THE TOP IN THE FRAME BELOW WITH THE MATCHING NUMBER.

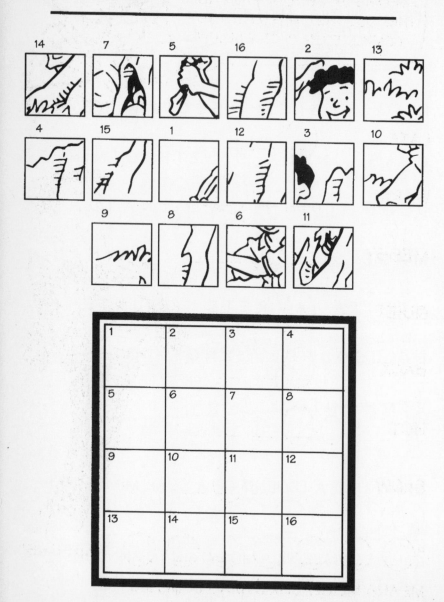

ALL JUMBLED UP

HEY . . . THIS ONE WILL BE FUN!
FIND THE OPPOSITE OF EACH WORD,
THEN USE THE CIRCLED LETTERS TO
COMPLETE THE PUZZLE BELOW.

LATE Ⓞ _ _ _ _

WARM _ _ Ⓞ _ _

MESSY _ Ⓞ _ _ _

QUIET Ⓞ _ _ _

BACK Ⓞ _ _ _

HOT Ⓞ _ _ _

SLOW _ _ Ⓞ _ _

"Ⓞ Ⓞ Ⓞ Ⓞ Ⓞ Ⓞ Ⓞ PASCUAS"

MEANS MERRY CHRISTMAS IN SPAIN.

139

WHERE ARE THOSE VOWELS?

YOU'RE GOING TO HAVE TO CONCENTRATE FOR THIS ONE! VOWELS ARE HIDDEN IN THE PICTURE BELOW. YOU WILL NEED THEM TO COMPLETE THE PUZZLE.

__N MEX__C__, THE N__NE DAYS BEF__RE CHR__STMAS ARE KN__WN AS THE P__SADA, WHERE__N, EVERY N__GHT, FAM__L__ES AND FR__ENDS J__ __N T__GETHER T__ F__ND A REF__GE F__R THE BABY JES__S. THEY HAVE A B__G PARTY __N THE LAST N__GHT, WHEN A REF__GE __S F__ __ND.

CAN YOU FIND THE WORDS?

ALL THESE
WORDS ARE HIDDEN IN
THE PUZZLE BELOW.
HAVE FUN!

FRIENDS   REFUGE
FAMILY   POSADA
PINATA   SEARCH
FEAST   MARIACHI
MEXICO   HORN

```
          J  S           N  T  K
    C  P  S  K  G  F  H  S  V  B  F        N  C
    N  E  D  Q  M  A  R  I  A  C  H  I  V
       A  R  Z  E  E  M  P  S  T  R  J  F
       F  R  K  F  G  W  X  I  K  H  A  M
    G  L  C  X  U  T  M  F  K  L  D  W  L
    W  M  H  F  R  S  Z  L  Q  A  Y  D  Z
    H  X  E  B  L  D  G  T  S  B  H  X  N  T
    Q  R  P  X  K  S  K  O  D  G  J  O  C  S
       M  K  J  I  V  P  R  N  D  H  L  R  V
    T  C  T  Z  C  W  P  E  Z  M  W  P  N
          M  B  N  O  P  I  N  A  T  A  D
          R  Q  X  K  C  R  J  V  F  Q
          B  G     S  F  H  B  T  L
```

141

UP OR DOWN?

UNSCRAMBLE THE WORDS, THEN IT'S UP TO YOU TO FIND WHERE EACH WORD GOES. WE PUT A FEW LETTERS IN TO HELP.

SDAOPA _____

RELCETAOBNI _____

NTAAIP _____

_____

EUSSJ _____

DANYC _____

EPSI _____

GFUERE _____

TNSU _____

THE CHRISTMAS GREETING IN MEXICO IS, "FELIZ NAVIDAD."

CAN YOU FIND THE WORDS?

ALL THESE WORDS ARE HIDDEN IN THE PUZZLE BELOW. HAVE FUN!

CANDY
TOYS
TREASURE
STICK
PARTY

NINE
BIBLICAL
POTTERY
HORSE
CHILDREN

```
          P   F   X
      H N I N E               J
      P O T T E R Y       B G
  L N H C B P G D N F L S
  B J R M C R A V H K Y
  S F T K H J B R M O S       T
      T R G I P I L T W R Q C
  H   E R L C B Q S Y V S K
  Q C C A N D Y L T C L P N E
  T M V S H R Q I F H J R K X
  K Z U W E N C V D W C G
  P D R H N P A B T I S D
  N E L S K L R T H L Z
      M B F Q D S G M J
```

LETTER CLUES

TO DECODE THIS MESSAGE, YOU'LL NEED TO TAKE THE LETTER FROM EACH NUMBERED CLUE AND MATCH IT TO THE NUMBERED SPACE IN THE PUZZLE BELOW.

1. THIS LETTER IS FOUND IN *SAND* BUT NOT IN *LAND*.

   _____

2. IT APPEARS ONCE IN *BALL* AND TWICE IN *PASTA*.

   _____

3. THIS LETTER BEGINS THE WORD *LORD* AND *LANE*.

   _____

4. IT'S FOUND IN *FATTER* BUT NOT IN *MATTER*.

   _____

5. THIS LETTER IS FOUND IN *YARN* BUT NOT IN *BARN*.

   _____

_ _THOUGH THE_ DO NOT CE_EBR_TE
2 3   5   3   2
CHRI_TM_ _ _ IN I_R_E_, THE_ DO
     1 2 1   1 2 3   5
H_VE _N IMPORT_NT HO_ID_ _ _ _T
 2   2   2   2   3 2 5   2
THI_ TIME O_ THE _E_R. IT I_
   1   4   5 2   1
C_ _ _ _ED, "H_NUKK_H", _ND IT I_
 2 3 3   4   5   2   2   1 1
_ _ _ _O KNOWN _ _ THE _E_TIV_
2 3 1   2 1   4 1   2 3
O_ _IGHT_ _ND I_ REPRE_ENTED B_
 4 3   1 2   1   5
_N EIGHT-BR_NCH MENOR_H, OR
2   1   2
C_ND_E HO_DER. IT CE_EBR_TE_
 2   3   3   3   2   1 2
MIR_C_E O_ _ONG _GO WHEN THE
   2 3   4   3   2
OI_, ON_ _ ENOUGH TO BURN _OR
   3   3 5   4
ONE D_ _ IN _ _ _ _MP, _ _ _TED
      2 5   3 2   3 2 1
OR EIGHT D _ _!
4   2 5 1

LESS SHALL BE FIRST

PLACE THE WORDS BELOW INTO THE PUZZLE ACCORDING TO THE NUMBER OF LETTERS IN EACH WORD, BEGINNING WITH THE WORD THAT HAS THE FEWEST LETTERS. THEN, UNSCRAMBLE THE CIRCLED LETTERS TO COMPLETE THE ANSWER BELOW.

CHRISTMAS   EIGHT
LIGHTS   HISTORICAL
HANUKKAH   MENORAH

I LOVE HANUKKAH!

POTATO PANCAKES OR ◯ ◯ ◯ ◯ ◯ ◯

ARE A FAVORITE DISH AT HANUKKAH.

LET'S MAZE AROUND

GET THROUGH THE TEMPLE TO LIGHT THE MENORAH FOR HANUKKAH.

FIND THE FOUR

COMPLETE THE PUZZLE BELOW BY CROSSING OUT EVERY LETTER THAT APPEARS AT LEAST FOUR TIMES. USE THE REMAINING LETTERS TO COMPLETE THE SENTENCE.

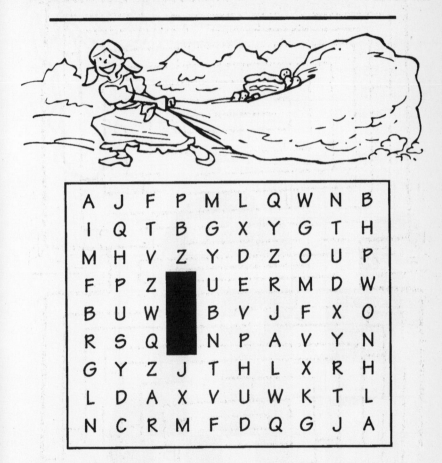

A	J	F	P	M	L	Q	W	N	B
I	Q	T	B	G	X	Y	G	T	H
M	H	V	Z	Y	D	Z	O	U	P
F	P	Z		U	E	R	M	D	W
B	U	W		B	V	J	F	X	O
R	S	Q		N	P	A	V	Y	N
G	Y	Z	J	T	H	L	X	R	H
L	D	A	X	V	U	W	K	T	L
N	C	R	M	F	D	Q	G	J	A

IN THE VILLAGE OF HALLWIL, IN SWITZERLAND, A YOUNG GIRL DRESSES AS THE CHRISTMAS CHILD OR, "WIENECTCHIND," AND VISITS FAMILIES, GIVING CAKES AND _ _ _ _ _ _ _ TO CHILDREN.

UP OR DOWN?

UNSCRAMBLE THE WORDS, THEN IT'S UP TO YOU TO FIND WHERE EACH WORD GOES. WE PUT A FEW LETTERS IN TO HELP.

LAORCS _____

RSESD _____   I NBU _____

GILLAEV _____   BROE _____

ZADRWNETISL   ERSO _____

_____   LEBLS _____

RNTAELN _____   NLOE _____

148

CAN YOU FIND THE WORDS?

ALL THESE
WORDS ARE HIDDEN IN
THE PUZZLE BELOW.
HAVE FUN!

WHITE
COLORED
SING
COOKIE
CAKE
SPIRIT

SWITZERLAND
LAMP
VILLAGE
CHILD
DECEMBER
SKIRT

```
      C P B F
    C L M H J D H V
  T G A C N I M N S
  J L Q K Z G L P W K
  F Q R V E B Q D I L
  M S V T R H F P T B
  S P I R I T J C Z R
  P H L N N V H D E S
  W D L K G M T E R K
  M H A L C Q I R L I
  D Q G P R K G N A R
  B J E K O F M J N T
  F L G C O L O R E D L G
C K D E C E M B E R B K D C
```

149

PICTURE MAKER

YOU MAKE THE PICTURE. DRAW THE IMAGE FROM EACH FRAME AT THE TOP IN THE FRAME BELOW WITH THE MATCHING NUMBER.

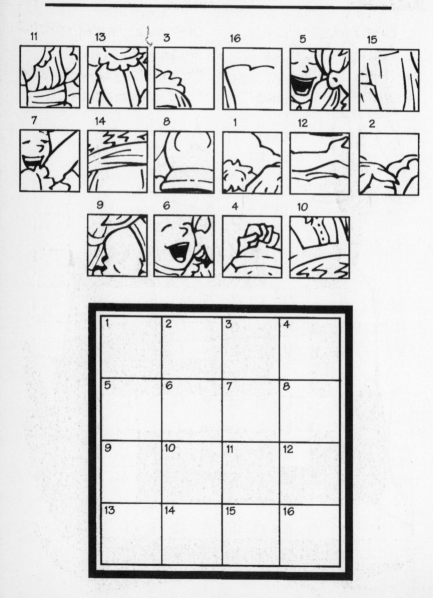

JUST A REGULAR OLD CROSSWORD!

ACROSS

1. GIVEN TO EACH OTHER
2. BOILED FOR DINNER
3. CHRISTMAS PLAY
4. WARM CAVITY IN HOME

DOWN

1. LIKE SPAIN AND NEXT DOOR
2. SALTED DRY FISH
3. BROUGHT IN FROM OUTSIDE
4. ALSO HOLDS PRESENTS

PICTURE MAKER

YOU MAKE THE PICTURE. DRAW THE IMAGE FROM EACH FRAME AT THE TOP IN THE FRAME BELOW WITH THE MATCHING NUMBER.

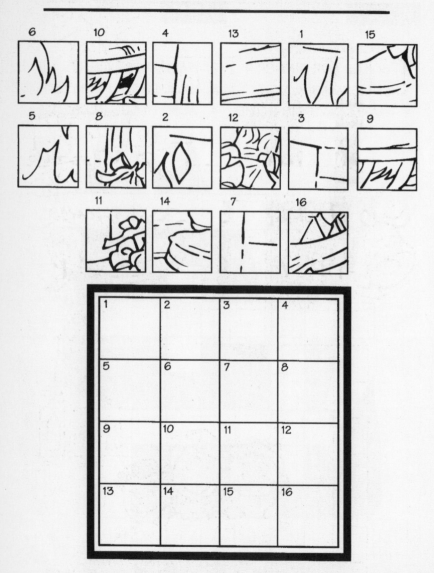

"BOAS FESTAS" IS PORTUGUESE FOR MERRY CHRISTMAS.

PICTURE CLUES

THE PICTURES ARE YOUR ONLY CLUES TO COMPLETING THIS CROSSWORD. THIS IS A BIT OF A BRAIN TEASER.

MERRY CHRISTMAS
FROM ALL OVER THE WORLD!

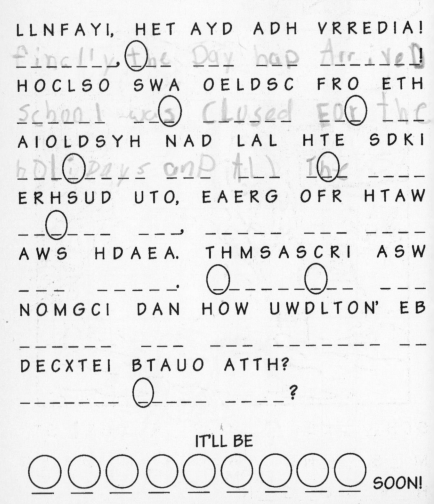

WHERE ARE THOSE VOWELS?

YOU'RE GOING TO HAVE TO CONCENTRATE FOR THIS ONE! VOWELS ARE HIDDEN IN THE PICTURE BELOW. YOU WILL NEED THEM TO COMPLETE THE PUZZLE.

SCH__O__O__L'S __O__U__T FOR CHR__Y__ST-M__A__S, __A__ND TH__E__ H__O__L__I__D__A__YS H__A__V__E__ B__E__G__U__N!

TRAVELLIN' RHYMES

THIS IS A GREAT GAME TO PLAY AS YOU TRAVEL. YOU'LL NEED SOMEONE TO PLAY IT WITH, THOUGH, LIKE YOUR BROTHER OR SISTER OR FRIENDS.

BELOW IS A LIST OF WORD PAIRS THAT RHYME WITH EACH OTHER. YOUR JOB IS TO CALL OUT THE WORDS AND HAVE THE PLAYERS COME UP WITH THE SILLIEST RHYMES. WRITE THE BEST ON THE SPACES BELOW.

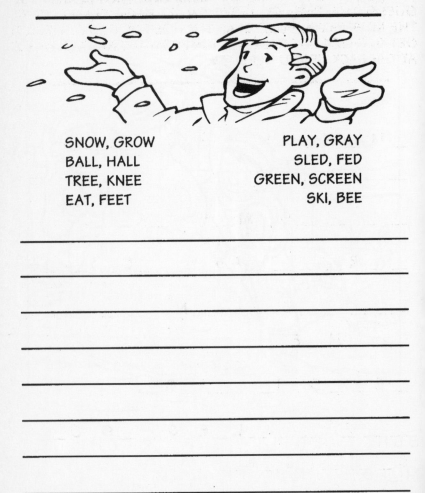

SNOW, GROW   PLAY, GRAY
BALL, HALL   SLED, FED
TREE, KNEE   GREEN, SCREEN
EAT, FEET   SKI, BEE

It's a Mystery

THIS IS A GREAT GAME TO PLAY AS YOU TRAVEL. YOU'LL NEED SOMEONE TO PLAY IT WITH, THOUGH, LIKE YOUR BROTHER OR SISTER OR FRIENDS.

BELOW IS A LIST OF PHRASES THAT NEED TO BE COMPLETED. SHOW THIS PUZZLE TO EACH PLAYER, WHO PICKS A LETTER TO FILL IN THE BLANKS, AND THEN HAS TEN SECONDS TO GUESS THE PHRASE. MOVE ON TO EACH PLAYER UNTIL THE MYSTERY IS SOLVED! AS THE HOST OF THIS GAME, YOU GET TO CHECK OUT THE SOLUTION FROM THE ANSWER PAGES AT THE BACK (IF YOU NEED TO)!

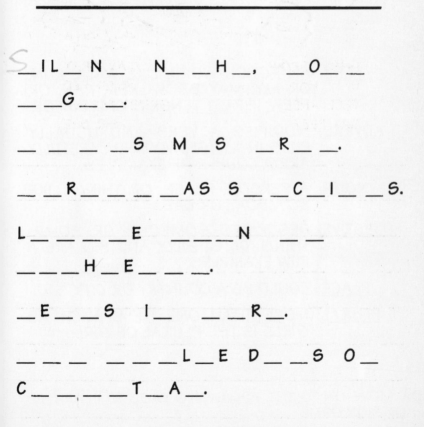

S _ I L _ N _   N _ _ H _ ,   _ O _ _

_ _ G _ _ .

_ _ _ _ _ S _ M _ S   _ R _ _ .

_ _ R _ _ _ _ A S   S _ _ C _ I _ _ S .

L _ _ _ _ E   _ _ _ N   _ _

_ _ _ H _ E _ _ _ .

_ E _ _ S   I _   _ _ R _ .

_ _ _   _ _ _ L _ E   D _ _ S   O _

C _ _ , _ _ T _ A _ .

REALLY SILLY STORIES

YOU CAN PLAY THIS GAME BY YOURSELF, BUT IT'S A LOT MORE FUN TO PLAY WITH OTHERS.

ASK EACH PLAYER TO CALL OUT THE KIND OF WORD INDICATED IN EACH SPACE—A NOUN OR ADJECTIVE OR ADVERB, FOR EXAMPLE—AND PLACE THAT WORD IN THE APPROPRIATE SPACE. DO NOT TELL ANYONE WHAT THE STORY IS ABOUT— IT'S MORE FUN THAT WAY!

BELOW YOU'LL FIND A DESCRIPTION OF WHAT VERBS, NOUNS, ADJECTIVES, ADVERBS, ETC., ARE—JUST IN CASE YOU NEED A LITTLE HELP.

<u>VERB:</u> AN ACTION WORD, LIKE *WALK, RUN,* OR *FLY.* MAY BE *WALKED, RAN,* OR *FLEW,* IF <u>PAST TENSE</u> IS CALLED FOR.

<u>ADVERB:</u> MODIFIES A VERB AND USUALLY ENDS IN "LY." *SLOWLY* AND *CAREFULLY* ARE A COUPLE OF EXAMPLES.

<u>NOUN:</u> A PERSON, PLACE, OR THING, LIKE *BOY, BOAT,* OR *CAR.*

<u>ADJECTIVE:</u> DESCRIBES SOMEONE OR SOME-THING. *DIRTY, SILLY,* AND *BIG* ARE A FEW EXAMPLES.

<u>PLACE:</u> COULD BE A *COUNTRY* OR *CITY,* ETC.

<u>PLURAL:</u> MORE THAN ONE ITEM, SUCH AS *GIRLS* IS THE PLURAL OF *GIRL.*

NOW MOVE ON TO THE FOLLOWING PAGE TO PLAY THIS REALLY SILLY GAME!

REALLY SILLY STORIES

DON'T LOOK AT THE STORY BELOW. INSTEAD, FILL IN THE BLANKS IN THE LIST BELOW WITH THE REQUIRED WORDS. THEN FILL IN THE BLANKS IN THE STORY AND GET READY TO LAUGH UNCONTROLLABLY!

_____

VERB—PAST TENSE _____

NOUN _____

NOUN _____

NOUN _____

NOUN _____

VERB _____

NOUN _____

NOUN _____

ADJECTIVE _____

NOUN _____

NOUN _____

TIME OF DAY _____

ADJECTIVE _____

NAME OF SEASON _____

NOUN _____

VERB—PAST TENSE _____

PLURAL NOUN _____

ADVERB _____

NOUN _____

NOUN _____

VERB—PAST TENSE _____

NOUN _____

VERB _____

WAYNE _____ ALL THE WAY _____ FROM SCHOOL. _____
   VERB (PAST TENSE)   NOUN   NOUN
WAS THE FIRST _____ OF THE _____ HOLIDAY AND HE
        NOUN   NOUN
COULD HARDLY _____ TO GET _____ AND PREPARE FOR THE
       VERB   NOUN
_____ THAT WAS _____. HE HEARD LAST _____ THAT IT
NOUN   ADJECTIVE   NOUN
WAS EVEN SUPPOSED TO _____ LATER IN THE
               NOUN
_____! NOW, WASN'T THAT JUST _____? HE HAD
 TIME OF DAY   ADJECTIVE
ALL HIS _____ GEAR TO GET OUT OF _____ AND
   NAME OF SEASON   NOUN
GET READY; HE _____ TO BE READY WHEN THE _____
     VERB (PAST TENSE)   PLURAL NOUN
WERE _____ WITH THAT WONDERFUL _____ STUFF. HE
   ADVERB   NOUN
NEEDED TO HAVE HIS _____ AND SKIS AND SNOW-
       NOUN
BOARD _____ AND WAXED AND READY FOR _____.
 VERB (PAST TENSE)   NOUN
HOW WOULD HE EVER BE ABLE TO _____ TONIGHT?
       VERB

CAN YOU FIND THE WORDS?

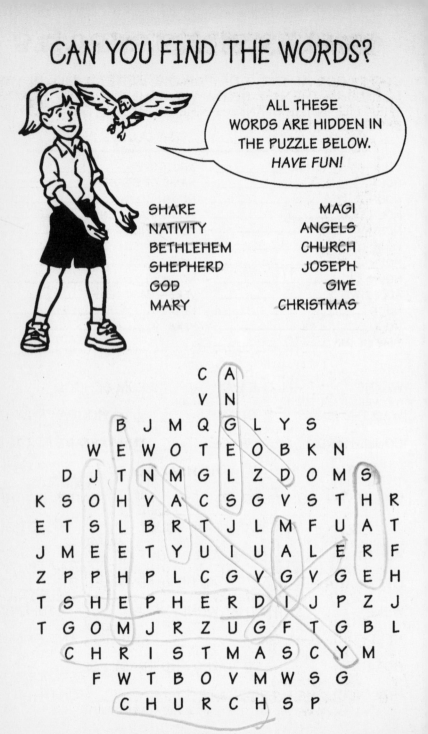

ALL THESE
WORDS ARE HIDDEN IN
THE PUZZLE BELOW.
HAVE FUN!

SHARE

NATIVITY

BETHLEHEM

SHEPHERD

GOD

MARY

MAGI

ANGELS

CHURCH

JOSEPH

GIVE

CHRISTMAS

PICTURE MAKER

YOU MAKE THE PICTURE. DRAW THE IMAGE FROM EACH FRAME AT THE TOP IN THE FRAME BELOW WITH THE MATCHING NUMBER.

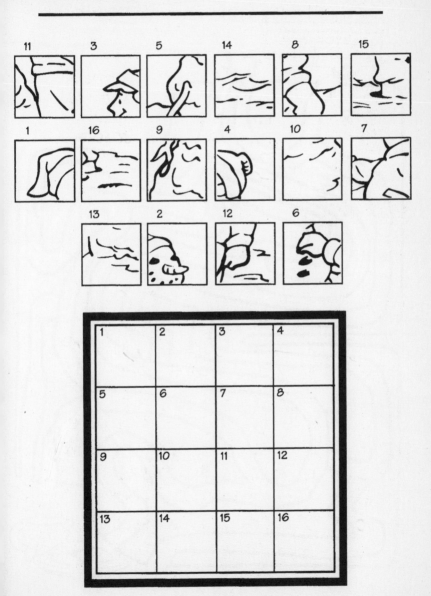

LET'S MAZE AROUND

SCHOOL'S OUT! HELP THE GANG GET HOME.

LESS SHALL BE FIRST

PLACE THE WORDS BELOW INTO THE PUZZLE ACCORDING TO THE NUMBER OF LETTERS IN EACH WORD, BEGINNING WITH THE WORD THAT HAS THE FEWEST LETTERS. THEN UNSCRAMBLE THE CIRCLED LETTERS TO COMPLETE THE ANSWER BELOW.

SNOWMAN   INSTRUCTOR
SPOON   PLAY
SHEPHERD   SCHOOL
GOD   CHRISTMAS

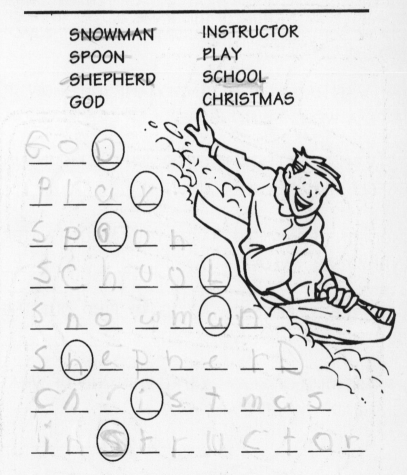

GOD
PLAY
SPOON
SCHOOL
SNOWMAN
SHEPHERD
CHRISTMAS
INSTRUCTOR

ENJOY THE

HOLIDAYS

163

WHO, WHAT, WHERE

THIS IS A GREAT GAME TO PLAY AS YOU TRAVEL. YOU'LL NEED SOMEONE TO PLAY IT WITH, THOUGH, LIKE YOUR BROTHER OR SISTER OR FRIENDS.

BELOW IS A LIST OF QUESTIONS THAT NEED A "WHO, WHAT, OR WHERE" ANSWER. EACH PLAYER HAS TEN SECONDS TO ANSWER. AS THE HOST OF THIS GAME, YOU GET TO CHECK OUT THE SOLUTION FROM THE ANSWER PAGES AT THE BACK (IF YOU NEED TO)!

THIS MAN HAS A LOT TO TEACH YOU IF YOU SHOW UP ONCE A WEEK. *WHO* IS HE?   Pastor

HE'LL SHOW YOU HOW TO GET DOWN THE MOUNTAIN SAFELY. *WHO* IS HE?   Ski instructor

IT DOESN'T FLY, AND IT MAKES YOUR MOUTH WATER EVERY YEAR. *WHAT* IS IT?   turkey

IT IS VERY DIFFICULT WAITING TO FIND OUT THE CONTENTS OF THIS. *WHAT* IS IT?   Gift

AT THIS TIME OF YEAR, YOU'RE THINKING OF WHAT IS AHEAD. *WHERE* ARE YOU?

School

FIND THE FOUR

COMPLETE THE PUZZLE BELOW BY CROSSING OUT EVERY LETTER THAT APPEARS AT LEAST FOUR TIMES. USE THE REMAINING LETTERS TO COMPLETE THE SENTENCE.

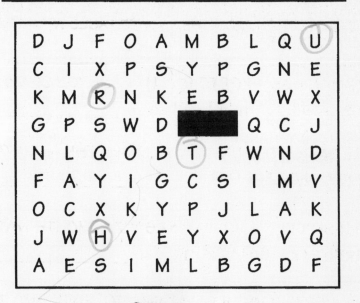

D	J	F	O	A	M	B	L	Q	U
C	I	X	P	S	Y	P	G	N	E
K	M	R	N	K	E	B	V	W	X
G	P	S	W	D	█	█	Q	C	J
N	L	Q	O	B	T	F	W	N	D
F	A	Y	I	G	C	S	I	M	V
O	C	X	K	Y	P	J	L	A	K
J	W	H	V	E	Y	X	O	V	Q
A	E	S	I	M	L	B	G	D	F

SNOWBALL FIGHTS ARE A LOT OF FUN, BUT TRY NOT TO _h_ _u_ _r_ _t_ ANYONE!

TRAVELLIN' RHYMES

THIS IS A GREAT GAME TO PLAY AS YOU TRAVEL. YOU'LL NEED SOMEONE TO PLAY IT WITH, THOUGH, LIKE YOUR BROTHER OR SISTER OR FRIENDS.

BELOW IS A LIST OF WORD PAIRS THAT RHYME WITH EACH OTHER. YOUR JOB IS TO CALL OUT THE WORDS AND HAVE THE PLAYERS COME UP WITH THE SILLIEST RHYMES. WRITE THE BEST ON THE SPACES BELOW.

BOOK, HOOK	LIVE, GIVE
EGG, BEG	SLEIGH, TRAY
CANDY, HANDY	ICE, MICE
SCHOOL, COOL	PLAY, STAY
FLAKE, RAKE	BAND, HAND

_____

_____

_____

_____

_____

_____

_____

_____

_____

JUST A REGULAR OLD CROSSWORD!

ACROSS

1. MUSIC PERFORMANCES
2. SNOW _____
3. FIRE BURNS IT
4. JUST LIKE SURFING
5. SEASONS MEANING
6. FISH THROUGH IT

DOWN

1. _____ HOLIDAY
2. SPECIAL SONGS
3. TEACHES ON MOUNTAIN
4. SKI _____
5. A SMALL TWIG
6. GOOD IN CABBAGE ROLLS

UP OR DOWN?

UNSCRAMBLE THE WORDS, THEN IT'S UP TO YOU TO FIND WHERE EACH WORD GOES. WE PUT A FEW LETTERS IN TO HELP.

ERTE _____

KURTYE _____

ENRTANSOM _____

NSRTEPE _____

HHBETELME _____

IANSGTK _____

A LITTLE FARTHER . . . AND YOU ARE *MINE!*

168

LETTER CLUES

TO DECODE THIS MESSAGE FROM GOD, YOU'LL NEED TO TAKE
THE LETTER FROM EACH NUMBERED CLUE AND MATCH IT TO
THE NUMBERED SPACE IN THE PUZZLE BELOW.

---

1. BEGINS THE WORD *NUT* AND ENDS THE WORD *MOON*.

   _____

2. APPEARS ONCE IN *ICE* AND TWICE IN *SKIING*.

   _____

3. THIS LETTER IS FOUND IN *BEGAN* BUT NOT IN *BEGUN*.

   _____

4. APPEARS TWICE IN *BOOT* BUT ONLY ONCE IN *POLE*.

   _____

5. FOUND TWICE IN BOTH *SNOWSHOE* AND *SOCKS*.

   _____

6. YOU'LL FIND THIS IN *LESS* BUT NOT IN *LOSS*.

   _____

7. BEGINS *TREE* AND IS IN THE MIDDLE OF *MOTOR*.

   _____

8. APPEARS ONCE IN *SISTER* AND TWICE IN *BROTHER*.

   _____

"Y_ U W_ LL B_ W_ _ H CH_ LD _ _ D
   4   2   6   2 7   2   3 1

G_ V_ B_ _ _ H _ _ _ _ _ _ _, _ _ D
 2 6   2 8 7   7 4 3 5 4 1   3 1

Y_ U _ _ _ _ _ G_ V_ H_ M _ H_
 4   3 8 6 7 4   2 6   2   7 6

_ _ M_ J_ _ U _."
1 3 6 6 5 5

LUKE 1:31

169

ALL JUMBLED UP

HEY . . . THIS ONE WILL BE FUN!
FIND THE *OPPOSITE* OF EACH WORD,
THEN USE THE CIRCLED LETTERS TO
COMPLETE THE PUZZLE BELOW.

SNOW — r a i n

UP — d o w n

RECEIVE — _ _ _ _

DARK — _ _ _ _ _

FULL — E m p t y

HAPPY — s a d

SISTER — B r o t h e r

CHRIST. THE TRUE

◯ ◯ ◯ ◯ ◯ ◯ ◯

OF CHRISTMAS.

170

DON'T LEAVE IT SCRAMBLED!

UNSCRAMBLE EACH WORD, THEN USE THE CIRCLED LETTERS TO COMPLETE THE PUZZLE BELOW . . . AND I HOPE IT DOESN'T HURT YOUR EYES!

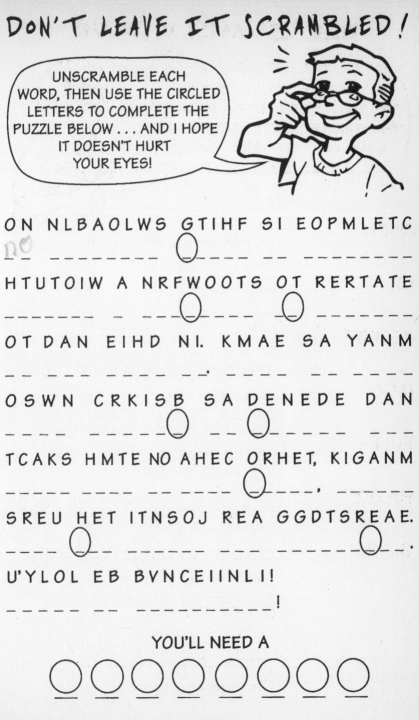

ON NLBAOLWS GTIHF SI EOPMLETC

__ _____ ◯____ __ _____

HTUTOIW A NRFWOOTS OT RERTATE

_____ _ ___◯___ __ ◯_____

OT DAN EIHD NI. KMAE SA YANM

__ ___ ____ __. ____ __ ____

OSWN CRKISB SA DENEDE DAN

____ ◯_____ __ ◯_____ ___

TCAKS HMTE NO AHEC ORHET, KIGANM

_____ ____ __ ◯___, _____

SREU HET ITNSOJ REA GGDTSREAE.

____ ◯__ _____ ___ ___◯____.

U'YLOL EB BVNCEIINL I!

_____ __ _____!

YOU'LL NEED A

◯ ◯ ◯ ◯ ◯ ◯ ◯ ◯
_ _ _ _ _ _ _ _

171

REALLY SILLY STORIES

YOU CAN PLAY THIS GAME BY YOURSELF, BUT IT'S A LOT MORE FUN TO PLAY WITH OTHERS.

ASK EACH PLAYER TO CALL OUT THE KIND OF WORD INDICATED IN EACH SPACE—A NOUN OR ADJECTIVE OR ADVERB, FOR EXAMPLE—AND PLACE THAT WORD IN THE APPROPRIATE SPACE. DO NOT TELL ANYONE WHAT THE STORY IS ABOUT— IT'S MORE FUN THAT WAY!

BELOW YOU'LL FIND A DESCRIPTION OF WHAT VERBS, NOUNS, ADJECTIVES, ADVERBS, ETC., ARE—JUST IN CASE YOU NEED A LITTLE HELP.

<u>VERB:</u> AN ACTION WORD, LIKE *WALK, RUN,* OR *FLY.* MAY BE *WALKED, RAN,* OR *FLEW,* IF <u>PAST TENSE</u> IS CALLED FOR.

<u>ADVERB:</u> MODIFIES A VERB AND USUALLY ENDS IN "LY." *SLOWLY* AND *CAREFULLY* ARE A COUPLE OF EXAMPLES.

<u>NOUN:</u> A PERSON, PLACE, OR THING, LIKE *BOY, BOAT,* OR *CAR.*

<u>ADJECTIVE:</u> DESCRIBES SOMEONE OR SOMETHING. *DIRTY, SILLY,* AND *BIG* ARE A FEW EXAMPLES.

<u>PLACE:</u> COULD BE A *COUNTRY* OR *CITY,* ETC.

<u>PLURAL:</u> MORE THAN ONE ITEM, SUCH AS *GIRLS* IS THE PLURAL OF *GIRL.*

NOW MOVE ON TO THE FOLLOWING PAGE TO PLAY THIS REALLY SILLY GAME!

REALLY SILLY STORIES

DON'T LOOK AT THE STORY BELOW. INSTEAD, FILL IN THE
BLANKS IN THE LIST BELOW WITH THE REQUIRED WORDS.
THEN FILL IN THE BLANKS IN THE STORY AND GET READY TO
LAUGH UNCONTROLLABLY!

VERB _____ ADJECTIVE _____

NOUN _____ NOUN _____

ADVERB _____ NOUN _____

NOUN _____ NOUN _____

ADJECTIVE _____ VERB (ENDING IN "ING")

ADJECTIVE _____

NOUN _____ NOUN _____

PLURAL NOUN _____ VERB (ENDING IN "ING")

VERB—PAST TENSE _____ _____

NOUN _____ NOUN _____

ADJECTIVE _____ ADJECTIVE _____

VERB _____ NOUN _____

PLURAL NOUN _____

FINALLY, THEY _____ AT THE TOP OF THE _____. THE DAY
　　　　　　　VERB　　　　　　　　　　　　　　NOUN

_____ WAS FULL OF _____, WITH THE _____ OF
ADVERB　　　　　　　　　NOUN　　　　　　　　ADJECTIVE

_____ RUNS DOWN FRESH _____. THEIR _____
ADJECTIVE　　　　　　　　　NOUN　　　　　　　PLURAL NOUN

WERE _____ AND POLISHED AND OFF SHE WENT. IT WAS AN
VERB (PAST TENSE)

EXHILARATING _____ AS THEY TACKLED THE _____ RUN OF
　　　　　　　NOUN　　　　　　　　　　ADJECTIVE

MANY THEY EXPECTED TO _____ THIS DAY. THEY KNEW
　　　　　　　　　　　　VERB

TO STAY OUT OF THE _____ MARKED _____ AND OFF-
　　　　　　　PLURAL NOUN　　　　　ADJECTIVE

LIMITS AND SO WOULD HAVE A _____ FILLED WITH _____ AND
　　　　　　　　　　　　　　NOUN　　　　　　　NOUN

_____. LATER, THEY LOOKED FORWARD TO _____ THEIR
NOUN　　　　　　　　　　　　　　　　VERB—"ING"

TIME UP AT THE _____, _____ IN FRONT OF THE _____
　　　　　　　NOUN　　VERB—"ING"　　　　　　　　NOUN

AND WARMING THEMSELVES WITH _____ HOT _____.
　　　　　　　　　　　　　ADJECTIVE　　　NOUN

TRAVELLIN' RHYMES

THIS IS A GREAT GAME TO PLAY AS YOU TRAVEL. YOU'LL NEED SOMEONE TO PLAY IT WITH, THOUGH, LIKE YOUR BROTHER OR SISTER OR FRIENDS.

BELOW IS A LIST OF WORD PAIRS THAT RHYME WITH EACH OTHER. YOUR JOB IS TO CALL OUT THE WORDS AND HAVE THE PLAYERS COME UP WITH THE SILLIEST RHYMES. WRITE THE BEST ON THE SPACES BELOW.

GLOVE, LOVE
BAKE, SNAKE
HORSE, COARSE
PLATE, GREAT

CAROL, BARREL
DINNER, THINNER
MEAT, FEET
SPELL, BELL

It's a Mystery

THIS IS A GREAT GAME TO PLAY AS YOU TRAVEL. YOU'LL NEED SOMEONE TO PLAY IT WITH, THOUGH, LIKE YOUR BROTHER OR SISTER OR FRIENDS.

BELOW IS A LIST OF PHRASES THAT NEED TO BE COMPLETED. SHOW THIS PUZZLE TO EACH PLAYER, WHO PICKS A LETTER TO FILL IN THE BLANKS, AND THEN HAS TEN SECONDS TO GUESS THE PHRASE. MOVE ON TO EACH PLAYER UNTIL THE MYSTERY IS SOLVED! AS THE HOST OF THIS GAME, YOU GET TO CHECK OUT THE SOLUTION FROM THE ANSWER PAGES AT THE BACK (IF YOU NEED TO)!

_ _ _ _H_ _E _ _ _E M_ _.

T_ _ _E_ W_ _ _ A_ _ T_E
_ _ _ _M_ _ G S.

_ _R_ _T, _ _ _ S_ _ _O_,
_ _ _ _R_.

_T_ B_ _T_R _ _ _ _ _ _
_ _AN _ _ _ _ _E_V_.

CH_ _ _T_ _ _ _ _ _.

_ _ _RY _ _ _ _ _S _ _AS A_D
A H_ _ _ _ _ _ _ _ _A_!

CAN YOU PICTURE IT?

THE PICTURES ARE YOUR CLUES. USE THE CIRCLED LETTERS TO COMPLETE THE PUZZLE BELOW.

WHAT'S REALLY, REALLY BIG AND COVERED WITH SNOW?

WHO, WHAT, WHERE

THIS IS A GREAT GAME TO PLAY AS YOU TRAVEL. YOU'LL NEED SOMEONE TO PLAY IT WITH, THOUGH, LIKE YOUR BROTHER OR SISTER OR FRIENDS.

BELOW IS A LIST OF QUESTIONS THAT NEED A "WHO, WHAT, OR WHERE" ANSWER. EACH PLAYER HAS TEN SECONDS TO ANSWER. AS THE HOST OF THIS GAME, YOU GET TO CHECK OUT THE SOLUTION FROM THE ANSWER PAGES AT THE BACK (IF YOU NEED TO)!

SKIS HELP GET YOU QUICKLY FROM THE TOP TO THE BOTTOM. *WHERE* ARE YOU? _____

THIS PERSON RECEIVED A MIRACLE, AND THE SAVIOR WAS BORN. *WHO* WAS IT? _____

THREE MEN FROM THE EAST VISITED THIS SMALL TOWN. *WHERE* WERE THEY? _____

IT IS MADE WAY UP NORTH, BUT YOU CAN MAKE ONE TOO. *WHAT* IS IT? _____

WITH THIS AND A HORSE YOU CAN *GO* ANYWHERE IN THE SNOW. *WHAT* IS IT? _____

ON THIS, YOU ENJOY THE SAME SPORT IN WINTER AND SUMMER. *WHAT* ARE THEY? _____

PICTURE MAKER

YOU MAKE THE PICTURE. DRAW THE IMAGE FROM EACH FRAME AT THE TOP IN THE FRAME BELOW WITH THE MATCHING NUMBER.

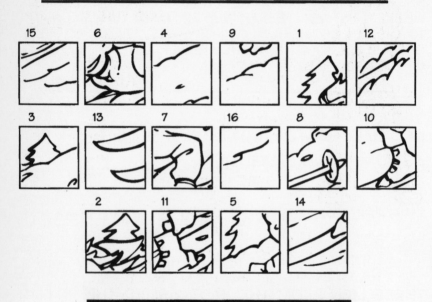

CAN YOU FIND THE WORDS?

ALL THESE
WORDS ARE HIDDEN IN
THE PUZZLE BELOW.
HAVE FUN!

ORNAMENT   JESUS
TREE   TURKEY
MANGER   CANDY
SNOWBALL   ICE
GIFTS   SCHOOL

```
            Y E
        S W C Q T U
    B H N I F P H S Y R
      Z O J L C V D F
    P T W T M N N Z L B
  F G U B K R A D T R E E
    M R A J C Z N G Z M
  Q Y K L T B E F G K H T
K S G E L Y M G J U E V T D
    U Y D A T R K E L R
  L C K N M Y N G P S W K
Z V Y R L S C H O O L U Q F
R N O F W Z C J G I F T S Y
            G S
```

COMPLETE THE PUZZLE BELOW BY CROSSING OUT EVERY LETTER THAT APPEARS AT LEAST FOUR TIMES. USE THE REMAINING LETTERS TO COMPLETE THE SENTENCE.

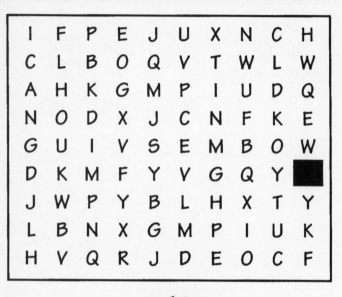

I	F	P	E	J	U	X	N	C	H
C	L	B	O	Q	V	T	W	L	W
A	H	K	G	M	P	I	U	D	Q
N	O	D	X	J	C	N	F	K	E
G	U	I	V	S	E	M	B	O	W
D	K	M	F	Y	V	G	Q	Y	■
J	W	P	Y	B	L	H	X	T	Y
L	B	N	X	G	M	P	I	U	K
H	V	Q	R	J	D	E	O	C	F

CHRISTMAS IS A TIME TO _ _ _ _ _

THINKING ABOUT OTHERS!

180

LESS SHALL BE FIRST

PLACE THE WORDS BELOW INTO THE PUZZLE ACCORDING TO THE NUMBER OF LETTERS IN EACH WORD, BEGINNING WITH THE WORD THAT HAS THE FEWEST LETTERS. THEN, UNSCRAMBLE THE CIRCLED LETTERS TO COMPLETE THE ANSWER BELOW.

DINNER

GIVE

HOLIDAYS

SKI

PRESENT

BETHLEHEM

IGLOO

TO YOU, A ___ ___ ___ ___ ___ ___ IS BORN.

181

REALLY SILLY STORIES

YOU CAN PLAY THIS GAME BY YOURSELF, BUT IT'S A LOT MORE FUN TO PLAY WITH OTHERS.

ASK EACH PLAYER TO CALL OUT THE KIND OF WORD INDICATED IN EACH SPACE—A NOUN OR ADJECTIVE OR ADVERB, FOR EXAMPLE—AND PLACE THAT WORD IN THE APPROPRIATE SPACE. DO NOT TELL ANYONE WHAT THE STORY IS ABOUT—IT'S MORE FUN THAT WAY!

BELOW YOU'LL FIND A DESCRIPTION OF WHAT VERBS, NOUNS, ADJECTIVES, ADVERBS, ETC., ARE—JUST IN CASE YOU NEED A LITTLE HELP.

VERB: AN ACTION WORD, LIKE *WALK*, *RUN*, OR *FLY*. MAY BE *WALKED*, *RAN*, OR *FLEW*, IF <u>PAST TENSE</u> IS CALLED FOR.

ADVERB: MODIFIES A VERB AND USUALLY ENDS IN "LY." *SLOWLY* AND *CAREFULLY* ARE A COUPLE OF EXAMPLES.

NOUN: A PERSON, PLACE, OR THING, LIKE *BOY*, *BOAT*, OR *CAR*.

ADJECTIVE: DESCRIBES SOMEONE OR SOMETHING. *DIRTY*, *SILLY*, AND *BIG* ARE A FEW EXAMPLES.

PLACE: COULD BE A *COUNTRY* OR *CITY*, ETC.

PLURAL: MORE THAN ONE ITEM, SUCH AS *GIRLS* IS THE PLURAL OF *GIRL*.

NOW MOVE ON TO THE FOLLOWING PAGE TO PLAY THIS REALLY SILLY GAME!

REALLY SILLY STORIES

DON'T LOOK AT THE STORY BELOW. INSTEAD, FILL IN THE BLANKS IN THE LIST BELOW WITH THE REQUIRED WORDS. THEN FILL IN THE BLANKS IN THE STORY AND GET READY TO LAUGH UNCONTROLLABLY!

NOUN _____

ADJECTIVE _____

PLURAL NOUN _____

VERB—PAST TENSE _____

VERB ENDING IN "ING"

_____

ADJECTIVE _____

VERB ENDING IN "ING"

_____

NOUN _____

PLURAL NOUN _____

NOUN _____

NOUN _____

NOUN _____

NOUN _____

PLURAL NOUN _____

NOUN _____

NOUN _____

PLURAL NOUN _____

NOUN _____

VERB _____

ADJECTIVE _____

PLURAL NOUN _____

ADJECTIVE _____

THE _____ WAS GETTING _____ AND HIGHER. KEVIN AND
   NOUN   ADJECTIVE

HIS THREE _____ HAD _____ THE MORNING _____ AN
        PLURAL NOUN VERB (PAST TENSE)   VERB—"ING"

_____ SNOW FORT AND WERE NOW _____ UP ON
ADJECTIVE   VERB—"ING"

THE "AMMUNITION" THEY WOULD NEED. WITH THE _____
                                            NOUN

OF _____ THEY WERE AMASSING, THE OTHER _____
    PLURAL NOUN   NOUN

WOULD HAVE NO _____ AGAINST THEM IN THIS _____
              NOUN   NOUN

_____ THAT WAS SURE TO MAKE HISTORY! BOTH _____
NOUN   PLURAL NOUN

HAD AGREED ON A _____ IT WOULD BEGIN, AND THAT LEFT
                NOUN

THEM AN _____ TO GO. AS THEY CONTINUED TO MAKE
        NOUN

_____ THEY DISCUSSED THEIR _____. THE OTHER GUYS
PLURAL NOUN   NOUN

WOULDN'T _____ A CHANCE! THEN, SUDDENLY A _____
       VERB   ADJECTIVE

OF _____ CAME AT THEM. IT WAS A _____ ATTACK!
    PLURAL NOUN   ADJECTIVE

PICTURE CLUES

THE PICTURES ARE YOUR ONLY CLUES TO COMPLETING THIS CROSSWORD. THIS IS A BIT OF A BRAIN TEASER.

LET'S MAZE AROUND

THE CHURCH PLAY HAS ALMOST BEGUN. HELP THE GANG
FIND THEIR WAY IN THE DARK.

DON'T LEAVE IT SCRAMBLED!

UNSCRAMBLE EACH WORD, THEN USE THE CIRCLED LETTERS TO COMPLETE THE PUZZLE BELOW ... AND I HOPE IT DOESN'T HURT YOUR EYES!

YVNREOEE ELVOS ICVEGERIN

_ _ _ _ _ _ _ _ _ _ _ _ _ _ _ _ _ _ _ _ _ _

FTIGS TA MRAHCTSSI NDA MEOS

_ _ _ _ _ _ _ _ _ _ _ _ _ _ _ _ _ _ _ _ _ _ _

VEHA NVEE ROSEEDVCDI HET OYJ

_ _ _ _ _ _ _ _ _ _ _ _ _ _ _ _ _ _ _ _ _ _ _ _

AHTT MESCO NI NIIGVG SGFTI.

_ _ _ _ _ _ _ _ _ _ _ _ _ _ _ _ _ _ _ _ _ _.

IHTS TUSMOC SI EASDB NO

_ _ _ _ _ _ _ _ _ _ _ _ _ _ _ _ _ _ _

GTFIS GOBRUTH OT HTE OWBENRN

_ _ _ _ _ _ _ _ _ _ _ _ _ _ _ _ _ _ _ _ _ _ _ _

EUSJS.

_ _ _ _ _.

_ _ _ _ _ _ _ _ _ _ OR MAGI,

KINGS FROM THE EAST, CARRIED GIFTS FOR THE LORD.

186

TRAVELLIN' RHYMES

THIS IS A GREAT GAME TO PLAY AS YOU TRAVEL. YOU'LL NEED SOMEONE TO PLAY IT WITH, THOUGH, LIKE YOUR BROTHER OR SISTER OR FRIENDS.

BELOW IS A LIST OF WORD PAIRS THAT RHYME WITH EACH OTHER. YOUR JOB IS TO CALL OUT THE WORDS AND HAVE THE PLAYERS COME UP WITH THE SILLIEST RHYMES. WRITE THE BEST ON THE SPACES BELOW.

MERRY, DAIRY	RABBIT, HABIT
TOYS, BOYS	SLIDE, HIDE
CAT, MAT	PINE, DINE
DEER, STEER	SING, RING

LET'S MAZE AROUND

THE KIDS HAVE BEEN OUT PLAYING ALL DAY, AND THEY ARE FAMISHED! THEY'VE JUST BEEN CALLED FOR DINNER—HELP THEM FIND THE SHORTEST WAY HOME.

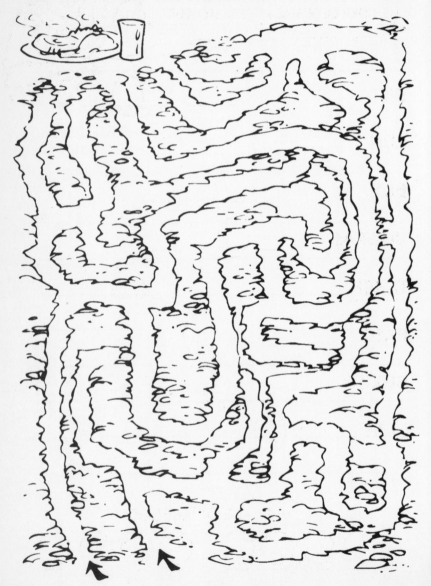

ALL JUMBLED UP

HEY . . . THIS ONE WILL BE FUN!
FIND THE OPPOSITE OF EACH WORD,
THEN USE THE CIRCLED LETTERS TO
COMPLETE THE PUZZLE BELOW.

SICK   _ _ _ _ Ⓞ _

RUN   Ⓞ _ _ _

BUY   Ⓞ _ _

UNWRAP   _ Ⓞ _ _

TEACH   _ _ _ _ Ⓞ

FAST   _ _ Ⓞ _

SHRINK   _ _ Ⓞ _

LAST   Ⓞ _ _ _

A PLACE OF REFUGE:

◯ ◯ ◯ ◯   ◯ ◯ ◯ ◯

189

REALLY SILLY STORIES

YOU CAN PLAY THIS GAME BY YOURSELF, BUT IT'S A LOT MORE FUN TO PLAY WITH OTHERS.

ASK EACH PLAYER TO CALL OUT THE KIND OF WORD INDICATED IN EACH SPACE—A NOUN OR ADJECTIVE OR ADVERB, FOR EXAMPLE—AND PLACE THAT WORD IN THE APPROPRIATE SPACE. DO NOT TELL ANYONE WHAT THE STORY IS ABOUT— IT'S MORE FUN THAT WAY!

BELOW YOU'LL FIND A DESCRIPTION OF WHAT VERBS, NOUNS, ADJECTIVES, ADVERBS, ETC., ARE—JUST IN CASE YOU NEED A LITTLE HELP.

<u>VERB:</u> AN ACTION WORD, LIKE *WALK, RUN,* OR *FLY.* MAY BE *WALKED, RAN,* OR *FLEW,* IF <u>PAST TENSE</u> IS CALLED FOR.

<u>ADVERB:</u> MODIFIES A VERB AND USUALLY ENDS IN "LY." *SLOWLY* AND *CAREFULLY* ARE A COUPLE OF EXAMPLES.

<u>NOUN:</u> A PERSON, PLACE, OR THING, LIKE *BOY, BOAT,* OR *CAR.*

<u>ADJECTIVE:</u> DESCRIBES SOMEONE OR SOMETHING. *DIRTY, SILLY,* AND *BIG* ARE A FEW EXAMPLES.

<u>PLACE:</u> COULD BE A *COUNTRY* OR *CITY,* ETC.

<u>PLURAL:</u> MORE THAN ONE ITEM, SUCH AS *GIRLS* IS THE PLURAL OF *GIRL.*

NOW MOVE ON TO THE FOLLOWING PAGE TO PLAY THIS REALLY SILLY GAME!

REALLY SILLY STORIES

DON'T LOOK AT THE STORY BELOW. INSTEAD, FILL IN THE BLANKS IN THE LIST BELOW WITH THE REQUIRED WORDS. THEN FILL IN THE BLANKS IN THE STORY AND GET READY TO LAUGH UNCONTROLLABLY!

NAME _molly_ PLURAL NOUN _mom's_
ADJECTIVE _carefully_ ADJECTIVE _Big_
NOUN _bike_ NOUN _car_
VERB (PAST TENSE) ADJECTIVE _Dairy_
meet NOUN _boat_
VERB _walking_ VERB (PAST TENSE)
NOUN _car_ _meet_
NOUN _Boy_ NOUN _Dads_
NOUN _Girl_ NOUN _Girl_
NOUN _Girl_ VERB _fly_
ADJECTIVE _silly_ ADJECTIVE _Big_
NOUN _car_

JEFFEREY AND _molly_ , ALONG WITH HER _carefully_
NAME   ADJECTIVE
bike , JIMMY HAD JUST _meet_ AT MAPLE TREE PARK
NOUN   VERB (PAST TENSE)
AND WERE BEGINNING THE LONG _walk_ UP THE WESTWARD
VERB
car . PULLING THE FRESHLY POLISHED _Boy_ BEHIND
NOUN   NOUN
THEM, THEY HAD IN MIND TO SPEND THE _Girl_ MAKING
NOUN
Girl DOWN THIS _silly_ HILL. THERE WERE FEW
NOUN   ADJECTIVE
mom's , AS IT WAS STILL _Big_ IN THE MORNING. AT
PLURAL NOUN   ADJECTIVE
LAST THEY ARRIVED AT THE _car_ AND DECIDED TO MOVE
NOUN
OVER _Dirty boat_ OR SO, AS ALONG THE WAY, THEY
ADJECTIVE   NOUN
HAD _meet_ A RATHER NASTY LOOKING _Dad_ UNDER
VERB (PAST TENSE)   NOUN
THE _Girl_ WHICH THEY WANTED TO _fly_ .
NOUN   VERB
FINALLY, THEY WERE OFF! WHAT A _Big_ _car_
ADJECTIVE   NOUN
THIS WAS GOING TO BE.

191

FIND THE FOUR

COMPLETE THE PUZZLE BELOW BY CROSSING OUT EVERY LETTER THAT APPEARS AT LEAST FOUR TIMES. USE THE REMAINING LETTERS TO COMPLETE THE SENTENCE.

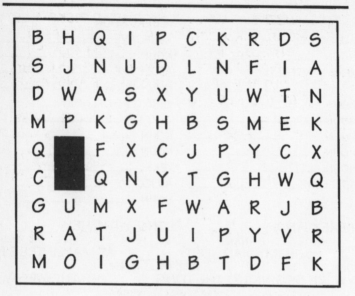

```
B H Q I P C K R D S
S J N U D L N F I A
D W A S X Y U W T N
M P K G H B S M E K
Q   F X C J P Y C X
C   Q N Y T G H W Q
G U M X F W A R J B
R A T J U I P Y V R
M O I G H B T D F K
```

JESUS WAS BORN BECAUSE OF GOD'S LOVE FOR YOU! IN HIM, YOU TOO CAN __ __ __ __ OTHERS.

it's a Mystery

THIS IS A GREAT GAME TO PLAY AS YOU TRAVEL. YOU'LL NEED SOMEONE TO PLAY IT WITH, THOUGH, LIKE YOUR BROTHER OR SISTER OR FRIENDS.

BELOW IS A LIST OF PHRASES THAT NEED TO BE COMPLETED. SHOW THIS PUZZLE TO EACH PLAYER, WHO PICKS A LETTER TO FILL IN THE BLANKS, AND THEN HAS TEN SECONDS TO GUESS THE PHRASE. MOVE ON TO EACH PLAYER UNTIL THE MYSTERY IS SOLVED! AS THE HOST OF THIS GAME, YOU GET TO CHECK OUT THE SOLUTION FROM THE ANSWER PAGES AT THE BACK (IF YOU NEED TO)!

_ _ E _ _ _ T _ E D _ _ _ M _ _ _ O _.

_ T _ _ _ _ _ _ _ H _ _ _ E _.

P _ _ _ E _ _ _ _ _ T _ A _ _ _ _ _ D _ I _ _ _ _ _ _ N.

_ _ _ _ _ _ _ _ _ G I _ _ _ A _ _ _ R.

_ H _ _ E _ _ _ _ _ _ T _ A _.

LETTER CLUES

TO DECODE THIS MESSAGE FROM *GOD*, YOU'LL NEED TO TAKE
THE LETTER FROM EACH NUMBERED CLUE AND MATCH IT TO
THE NUMBERED SPACE IN THE PUZZLE BELOW.

_____

1.   IT CAN BE FOUND IN *LAST* BUT NOT IN *LOST*.

_____

2.   LOOK FOR IT ONCE IN BOTH *TOY* AND IN *YELL*.

_____

3.   THIRD IN PLACE IN BOTH *RENT* AND IN *LENT*.

_____

4.   IT CAN BE FOUND IN *SONG* BUT NOT IN *SANG*.

_____

5.   IT DOUBLES BOTH *BOOTS* AND *TOBOGGANS*.

_____

6.   THIS LETTER BEGINS *ROUND* AND ENDS *HOUR*.

_____

7.   IT IS FOUND AT THE BEGINNING OF *JAM* AND *JOY*.

_____

"WHE _ THE _ _ _ W THE _ T _ _,
     3   2   5 1   5 1 6

THE _ WE _ E _ VE _ _ _ _ E D. _ _
   2   6   4 6 7 4 2   4 3

C _ MI _ G T _ THE H _ U _ E, THE _
 4   3   4   4 5   2

_ _ W THE CHILD WITH HI _ M _ THE _
5 1   5   4   6

M _ _ _, _ _ D THE _ B _ WED D _ W _
 1 6 2 1 3   2   4   4 3

_ _ D W _ _ _ HIPED HIM."
1 3   4 6 5

MATTHEW 2:10–11

194

CAN YOU FIND THE WORDS?

ALL THESE WORDS ARE HIDDEN IN THE PUZZLE BELOW. HAVE FUN!

SILENT
HOLY
CANDLE
CONCERT
HOLIDAY

TOYS
MOUNTAIN
BELLS
TINSEL
HOLLY

```
                              W  T  Y
         R  J  K  M  Y  K  S  Q  H  F  H
      T  R  Z  M  T  L  T  G  W  K  O  Z  O
   B  E  L  L  S  O  D  L  I  Z  B  L  S  L
   H  W  E  Q  H  K  U  Y  U  N  G  L  A  I
   Q  M  S  L  U  P  F  N  H  L  S  Y  H  D
   K  G  I  B  F  K  G  L  T  T  L  E  W  A
   D  Z  L  S  Q  T  V  J  R  A  Q  T  L  Y
   K  T  E  D  K  H  A  E  T  W  I  R  B  J
   C  A  N  D  L  E  C  P  E  V  E  R  N  U  W
   E  B  T  Q  F  N  K  Z  R  F  Q  D  G  L
   L  W  U  Y  O  G  W  M  S  L  B  N  Q  T
   M  P  F  C  E  J  L  W  F  T  P  G  Y  P
   S  G                    T  O  Y  S
```

CAN YOU PICTURE IT?

THE PICTURES ARE YOUR CLUES. USE THE CIRCLED LETTERS TO
COMPLETE THE PUZZLE BELOW.

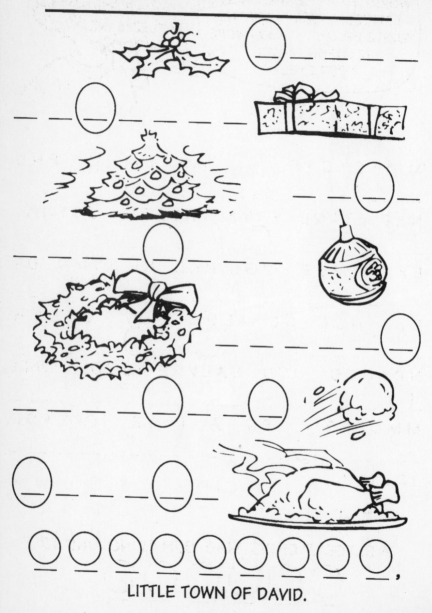

◯◯◯◯◯◯◯◯◯ ,

LITTLE TOWN OF DAVID.

DON'T LEAVE IT SCRAMBLED!

UNSCRAMBLE EACH WORD, THEN USE THE CIRCLED LETTERS TO COMPLETE THE PUZZLE BELOW . . . AND I HOPE IT DOESN'T HURT YOUR EYES!

MIRHSTCAS   SI   OS   CMHU   FNU

_ _ _ _ _ _ _ _ _   _ _   _ _   _ _ _ _   _ _ _

NAD EYRVE ERYA VAEESL IGSTNAL

_ _ _   _ _ _ _ _   _ _( )_   _ _ _ _ _ _   _ _ _ _ _

ERSIMMOE. PGEINKE NI DIMN OT

_ _ _ _ _ _ _.   _ _ _ _ _ _ _   _ _   _ _ _ _   _ _

EB   NCOTREAIEDS   OT   OTESH

_ _   _ _ _( )_ _ _ _ _( )_ _   _ _( )   _ _ _ _ _

NRAODU OYU SALVEE UYO HWTI

( )_ _ _ _ _   _ _ _   _ _ _ _ _   _ _ _   _ _ _ _

MMOEESIR FO A RVYE ICPEASL

_ _ _( )_ _ _ _   _ _   _   _ _ _ _   _ _ _ _ _ _ _

IDKN.

_ _ _ _.

A BLESSED CHRISTMAS IS IN BEING KIND TO

( ) ( ) ( ) ( ) ( ) ( )

_ _ _ _ _ _.

197

PICTURE MAKER

YOU MAKE THE PICTURE. DRAW THE IMAGE FROM EACH FRAME AT THE TOP IN THE FRAME BELOW WITH THE MATCHING NUMBER.

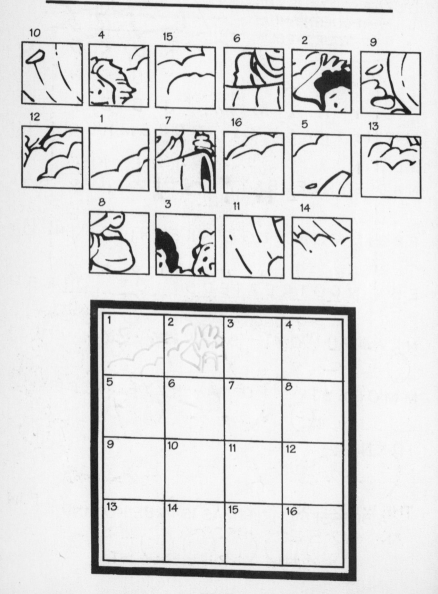

COMPLETE THE PUZZLE BELOW BY CROSSING OUT EVERY LETTER THAT APPEARS AT LEAST FOUR TIMES. USE THE REMAINING LETTERS TO COMPLETE THE SENTENCE.

N	H	I	S	T	P	K	V	R	D
A	L	Q	B	Z	W	X	U	S	N
P	W	Y	M			J	B	Z	L
D	O	J				A	W	Q	
N	X	K				P	A	B	
J	D	Z				F	S	V	
C	X	L	Y		D	I	Y	E	
V	B	S	P	G	Y	Z	I	N	K
K	Q	I	L	W	J	Q	V	A	X

THE WINTER SEASON IS FULL OF _ _ _ _ _ FUN
AND EXCITEMENT, BUT DON'T _ _ _ _ _ _
WHAT IT'S REALLY ABOUT.

REALLY SILLY STORIES

YOU CAN PLAY THIS GAME BY YOURSELF, BUT IT'S A LOT MORE FUN TO PLAY WITH OTHERS.

ASK EACH PLAYER TO CALL OUT THE KIND OF WORD INDICATED IN EACH SPACE—A NOUN OR ADJECTIVE OR ADVERB, FOR EXAMPLE—AND PLACE THAT WORD IN THE APPROPRIATE SPACE. DO NOT TELL ANYONE WHAT THE STORY IS ABOUT—IT'S MORE FUN THAT WAY!

BELOW YOU'LL FIND A DESCRIPTION OF WHAT VERBS, NOUNS, ADJECTIVES, ADVERBS, ETC., ARE—JUST IN CASE YOU NEED A LITTLE HELP.

VERB: AN ACTION WORD, LIKE *WALK*, *RUN*, OR *FLY*. MAY BE *WALKED*, *RAN*, OR *FLEW*, IF <u>PAST TENSE</u> IS CALLED FOR.

ADVERB: MODIFIES A VERB AND USUALLY ENDS IN "LY." *SLOWLY* AND *CAREFULLY* ARE A COUPLE OF EXAMPLES.

NOUN: A PERSON, PLACE, OR THING, LIKE *BOY*, *BOAT*, OR *CAR*.

ADJECTIVE: DESCRIBES SOMEONE OR SOMETHING. *DIRTY*, *SILLY*, AND *BIG* ARE A FEW EXAMPLES.

PLACE: COULD BE A *COUNTRY* OR *CITY*, ETC.

PLURAL: MORE THAN ONE ITEM, SUCH AS *GIRLS* IS THE PLURAL OF *GIRL*.

NOW MOVE ON TO THE FOLLOWING PAGE TO PLAY THIS REALLY SILLY GAME!

REALLY SILLY STORIES

DON'T LOOK AT THE STORY BELOW. INSTEAD, FILL IN THE BLANKS IN THE LIST BELOW WITH THE REQUIRED WORDS. THEN FILL IN THE BLANKS IN THE STORY AND GET READY TO LAUGH UNCONTROLLABLY!

NOUN _____   VERB (PAST TENSE)
ADJECTIVE _____   _____
NOUN _____   ADVERB _____
NOUN _____   NOUN _____
VERB ENDING IN "ING"   NOUN _____
_____   NOUN _____
NOUN _____   PLURAL NOUN _____
NOUN _____   PLURAL NOUN _____
ADJECTIVE _____   ADJECTIVE _____
NOUN _____   VERB _____
                         PLURAL NOUN _____

A __Dad__ OF __silly__ SNOW COVERED THE __park__
   NOUN   ADJECTIVE   NOUN

ON THIS CHRISTMAS __play__. CHILDREN WERE __running__
               NOUN   VERB—"ING"

IN EVERY __Car__ AND EACH WAS FILLED WITH AWE AND
          NOUN

__Boat__ AS THEY LOOKED __dirty__. WHAT A BEAUTIFUL
  NOUN   ADJECTIVE

__park__ THAT WOULD ACCOMPANY THEM AS THEY
  NOUN

__travels__ TO OPEN PRESENTS __slowly__ THIS
VERB (PAST TENSE)   ADVERB

__truck__. WHAT A WONDERFUL __baby__ TO BE SO
 NOUN   NOUN

BLESSED WITH __God__ AND PLENTY AND SECURITY. THEIR
           NOUN

__boys__ WOULD REMIND THEM THAT THERE WERE
PLURAL NOUN

SO MANY __babys__ NOT SO __big__ AND THAT
        PLURAL NOUN   ADJECTIVE

THEY SHOULD BE SURE TO __walke__ THEM IN MIND AND IN
                     VERB

THEIR __Girls__.
    PLURAL NOUN

JUST A REGULAR OLD CROSSWORD!

ACROSS

1. THINKING OF OTHERS
2. CHRISTMAS SCENE
3. TYPE OF TREE
4. CONSUMING FOOD
5. NICE TO WALK IN

DOWN

1. KIND TO OTHERS
2. TREE ORNAMENT
3. CHRISTMAS MEAT
4. TO STUMBLE
5. WIFE OF A CARPENTER

HERE ARE THE
ANSWERS!

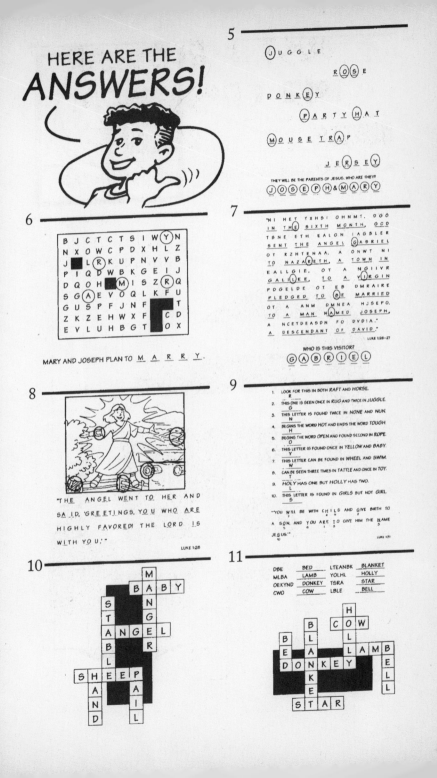

5

Ⓙ U G G L E

Ⓡ O S Ⓔ

D O N K Ⓔ Y

Ⓟ A R T Y Ⓗ A T

Ⓜ O U S E T R Ⓐ P

J Ⓔ R S Ⓔ Y

THEY WILL BE THE PARENTS OF JESUS. WHO ARE THEY?

Ⓙ Ⓞ S Ⓔ Ⓟ Ⓗ & Ⓜ Ⓐ R Ⓨ

6

```
B J C T C T S I W Ⓨ Ⓝ
N X O W C P D X H L Z
J ■ L Ⓡ K U P N V V B
P I Q D W B K G E I J
D Q O H Ⓜ I S Z Ⓡ Q
S Ⓖ Ⓐ E V O Q L K F U
G U S P F J N F ■ ■ T
Z K Z E H W X F ■ C D
E V L U H B G T ■ O X
```

MARY AND JOSEPH PLAN TO M A R R Y .

7

"NI HET TXH5I OHNMT. OGO
IN THE SIXTH MONTH, GOD
T5NE ETH EALGN IAGBLER
SENT THE ANGEL GⒶBRIEL
OT RZHTENAA. A ONWT NI
TO NAZAⓇETH, A TOWN IN
EALLGIE, OT A NGIIVR
GALILEE, TO A VⒾRGIN
PDGELDE OT EB DMRAIRE
PLEDGED TO ⒷE MARRIED
OT A ANM DMNEA HJ5EPO.
TO A MAN NⒶMED JOSEPH,
A NCETDEA5DN FO DVDIA."
A DESCENDANT OF DAVID."
LUKE 1:26-27

WHO IS THIS VISITOR?

Ⓖ Ⓐ Ⓑ Ⓡ Ⓘ Ⓔ L

8

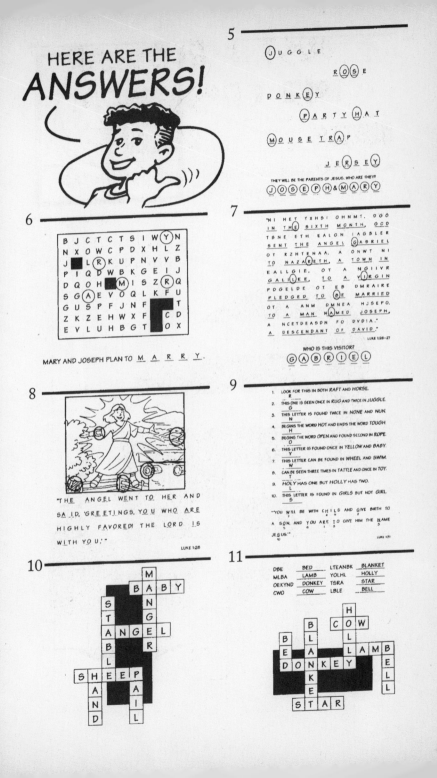

"THE ANGEL WENT TO HER AND
SAID, 'GREETINGS, YOU WHO ARE
HIGHLY FAVORED! THE LORD IS
WITH YOU.'"
LUKE 1:28

9

1. LOOK FOR THIS IN BOTH RAFT AND HORSE.
   R
2. THIS ONE IS SEEN ONCE IN RUG AND TWICE IN JUGGLE.
   G
3. THIS LETTER IS FOUND TWICE IN NONE AND NUN.
   N
4. BEGINS THE WORD HOT AND ENDS THE WORD TOUGH.
   H
5. BEGINS THE WORD OPEN AND FOUND SECOND IN ROPE.
   O
6. THIS LETTER IS FOUND ONCE IN YELLOW AND BABY.
   Y
7. THIS LETTER CAN BE FOUND IN WHEEL AND SWIM.
   W
8. CAN BE SEEN THREE TIMES IN TATTLE AND ONCE IN TOY.
   T
9. HOLY HAS ONE BUT HOLLY HAS TWO.
   L
10. THIS LETTER IS FOUND IN GIRLS BUT NOT GIRL.
    S

"YOU WILL BE WITH CHILD AND GIVE BIRTH TO
A SON, AND YOU ARE TO GIVE HIM THE NAME
JESUS."
LUKE 1:31

10

```
        M
      B A B Y
    S   N
    T   G
    A N G E L
    B   R
    L
  S H E E P
    A       A
    N       I
    D       L
```

11

DBE	BED	LTEANBK	BLANKET
MLBA	LAMB	YOLHL	HOLLY
OEKYND	DONKEY	T5RA	STAR
CWO	COW	LBLE	BELL

```
        H
      B   C O W
  B   L   L
  E   A   L
  D O N K E Y   L A M B
      K         E
      E         L
      S T A R   L
```

12

```
H K F T O R P J Y V M
N V Q Z C W G V M E S
P B A S V Q U T Z E K
U X M          Z L R
G E O          O P W
S N T J F G X Z B Y F
D R Q I K R S A W J U
J Y U P N M O G N Q B
A T F W E B X A K Y X
```

MARY FINDS OUT THAT HER COUSIN, ELIZABETH,
WILL ALSO HAVE A C H I L D .

14

15

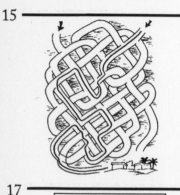

16

```
                    Y J
                  J K
   S D W K G F L R K F I W G P
   T C H I L D H N U N D C
   A A S H N B P W S G H A A
   X F R D T N B L D J B M
   Q G D P S V H I O W V E L
   H E N W       L E F   N C
   E W O W       J U S   C H
   R N B F       G U I N B R P
   O F R D       O Y I D V I W I
   D T R T       R T R E E G F
   T D         R T H A T D
   Z F G A L I L E E M A O S M
```

17

"WHEN ELIZABETH HEARD
MARY'S GREETING, THE BABY
LEAPED IN HER WOMB, AND
ELIZABETH WAS FILLED
WITH THE HOLY SPIRIT."

LUKE 1:41

20

"SCBEAEU SHEOJP RHE DSBHNUA
"BECAUSE JOSEPH HER HUSBAND

SWA A OGRIUHSTE ANM DAN
WAS A RIGHTEOUS MAN AND

IDD TNO TANW OT PSXOEE RHE
DID NOT WANT TO EXPOSE HER

OT UCLPIB AIGERDSC, EH DHA NI
TO PUBLIC DISGRACE HE HAD IN

DMNI OT RVOECDI EHR YUQLITE."
MIND TO DIVORCE HER QUIETLY."

MATTHEW 1:19

WHAT DID JOSEPH PLAN TO DO ABOUT THE WEDDING?

C A N C E L

21

THE LORD JESUS WAS BORN
IN BETHLEHEM.

THE MAGI BROUGHT GIFTS.

THERE WAS NO ROOM AT
THE INN.

A GREAT HOST OF ANGELS
APPEARED.

MARY, THE MOTHER OF THE
BABY JESUS.

A CHILD IS BORN, WHO
IS CHRIST, THE LORD.

22

M A S K

B L A N K E T

S W I N G

B I P L A N E

L A M P

S U N H A T

WHO FOLLOWED THE STAR?

M A G I FROM THE E A S T

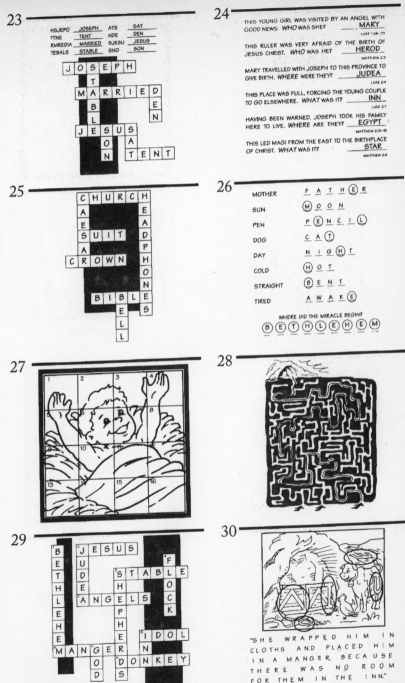

23

HSJEPO	JOSEPH	ATS	SAT
TTNE	TENT	NDE	DEN
RMREDIA	MARRIED	SJESU	JESUS
TEBALS	STABLE	SNO	SON

Crossword:
J O S E P H
T
M A R R I E D
E
J E S U S
O N
T E N T

24

THIS YOUNG GIRL WAS VISITED BY AN ANGEL WITH GOOD NEWS. *WHO* WAS SHE? ___ MARY
LUKE 1:26-33

THIS RULER WAS VERY AFRAID OF THE BIRTH OF JESUS CHRIST. *WHO* WAS HE? ___ HEROD
MATTHEW 2:3

MARY TRAVELLED WITH JOSEPH TO THIS PROVINCE TO GIVE BIRTH. *WHERE* WERE THEY? ___ JUDEA
LUKE 2:4

THIS PLACE WAS FULL, FORCING THE YOUNG COUPLE TO GO ELSEWHERE. *WHAT* WAS IT? ___ INN
LUKE 2:7

HAVING BEEN WARNED, JOSEPH TOOK HIS FAMILY HERE TO LIVE. *WHERE* ARE THEY? ___ EGYPT
MATTHEW 2:13-15

THIS LED MAGI FROM THE EAST TO THE BIRTHPLACE OF CHRIST. *WHAT* WAS IT? ___ STAR
MATTHEW 2:9

25

Crossword:
C H U R C H
A   E
E S U I T A
A   D
C R O W N P
         H
    B I B L E S
         E
         L
         L

26

MOTHER	F A T H (E) R
SUN	(M) O O N
PEN	P (E) N C I (L)
DOG	C A (T)
DAY	N I (G) (H) T
COLD	(H) O T
STRAIGHT	(B) E N T
TIRED	A W A (K) (E)

WHERE DID THE MIRACLE BEGIN?

(B) (E) (T) (H) (L) (E) (H) (E) (M)

27

28

29

Crossword:
B   J E S U S
E   U   F
T   D   S T A B L E
H   E   H   O
L   A N G E L S C
E   P   K
H   H   I D O L
E M A N G E R
        E D O N K E Y
        S

30

"SHE WRAPPED HIM IN CLOTHS AND PLACED HIM IN A MANGER, BECAUSE THERE WAS NO ROOM FOR THEM IN THE INN."
LUKE 2:7

31

1. THIS LETTER BEGINS *HAIR* AND ENDS *ROUGH*.
   H
2. FOUND SECOND TO LAST IN BOTH *LOVE* AND *LEAVE*.
   V
3. FOUND ONCE IN *CRUMB* AND TWICE IN *ACCEPT*.
   C
4. THIS ONE'S TWICE IN *EFFECT* BUT ONCE IN *FAIR*.
   F
5. YOU'LL FIND THIS ONE IN *BEST* BUT NOT IN *BUST*.
   E
6. YOU'LL FIND THIS TWICE IN *BABY* AND ONCE IN *BOAT*.
   B
7. THIS LETTER BEGINS *GOAT* AND ENDS *JOG*.
   G

"AND THERE WERE SHEPHERDS
LIVING OUT IN THE FIELDS NEARBY.
KEEPING WATCH OVER THEIR
FLOCKS AT NIGHT."

LUKE 2:8

32

33

AN A N G E L APPEARS TO THE SHEPHERDS.

34

ISHHGTE	HIGHEST	WCAHT	WATCH
ONTW	TOWN	5HTO	HOST
GYLRO	GLORY	DLGA	GLAD
VLNYEEAH	HEAVENLY	ISH	HIS
DLRO	LORD	AEHRT	EARTH
HNEOS	SHONE	ERATH	HEART

35

SHEPHERDS WERE AT WORK, LOOKING AFTER THEIR
SHEEP. *WHERE* WERE THEY? FIELDS
LUKE 2:8

SUDDENLY, SOMETHING SHONE ALL AROUND THEM.
WHAT WAS IT? GLORY OF THE LORD
LUKE 2:9

HE BROUGHT THEM GOOD NEWS OF GREAT JOY FOR
ALL PEOPLE. *WHO* WAS HE? ANGEL
LUKE 2:10

A SAVIOR HAD BEEN BORN WHO WAS CHRIST, THE
LORD. *WHERE* WAS HE BORN? TOWN OF DAVID
LUKE 2:11

ALL GLORY WAS GIVEN TO HIM BY THE ANGELS AND
ALL MEN. *WHO* WAS HE? GOD
LUKE 2:14

HE HAD NO BED, BUT THEY FOUND A PLACE TO LAY
HIM DOWN. *WHAT* WAS IT? MANGER
LUKE 2:12

PEACE WAS GIVEN TO THEM ON WHOM RESTED THE
FAVOR OF GOD. *WHO* WERE THEY? MEN
LUKE 2:14

36

37

"LDSUYNDE A RTEAG MCAYNOP FO
SUDDENLY A GREAT COMPANY OF

HET VHNEEAYL 5THO EEAARPDP WHTI
THE HEAVENLY HOST APPEARED WITH

ETH NEALG, IISPRGAN DGO NDA
THE ANGEL, PRAISING GOD AND

NASYGI, 'OGLRY OT ODG NI HET
SAYING, 'GLORY TO GOD IN THE

EIHSTGH, NAD NO TERAH ECPEA
HIGHEST. AND ON EARTH PEACE

OT NME NO OWMH ISH AFRVO
TO MEN ON WHOM HIS FAVOR

TRSES.'"
RESTS.'"

LUKE 2:13-14

THE HOST OF ANGELS
P R A I S E D GOD.

40

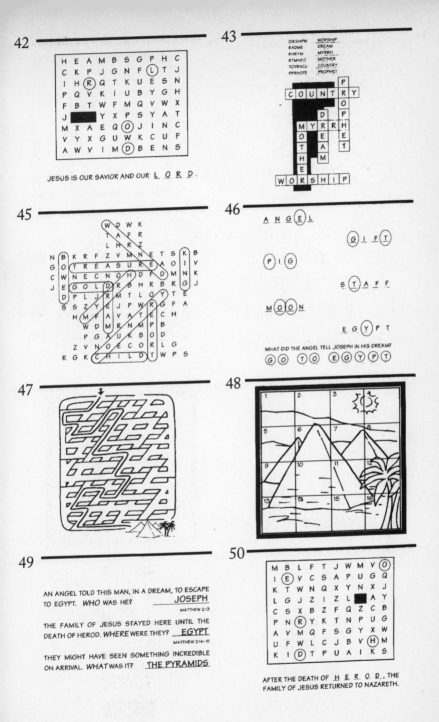

42

JESUS IS OUR SAVIOR AND OUR L O R D.

43

OIRSHPW — WORSHIP
RADME — DREAM
RHRYM — MYRRH
RTMHFO — MOTHER
TOYRNCU — COUNTRY
PPRHOTE — PROPHET

45

46

A N G E L

G I F T

P I G

S T A F F

M O O N

E G Y P T

WHAT DID THE ANGEL TELL JOSEPH IN HIS DREAM?
G O   T O   E G Y P T

47

48

49

AN ANGEL TOLD THIS MAN, IN A DREAM, TO ESCAPE
TO EGYPT. *WHO* WAS HE?   JOSEPH
MATTHEW 2:13

THE FAMILY OF JESUS STAYED HERE UNTIL THE
DEATH OF HEROD. *WHERE* WERE THEY?   EGYPT
MATTHEW 2:14-15

THEY MIGHT HAVE SEEN SOMETHING INCREDIBLE
ON ARRIVAL. *WHAT* WAS IT?   THE PYRAMIDS

50

AFTER THE DEATH OF H E R O D , THE
FAMILY OF JESUS RETURNED TO NAZARETH.

HERE ARE THE
ANSWERS!

54

THEY TRAVELLED A GREAT DISTANCE TO SEE A NEW-BORN KING. *WHO* WERE THEY? **MAGI**

IT IS A MESSAGE OF JOY AND COMES ONCE EVERY YEAR. *WHAT* IS IT? **CHRISTMAS**

IF THIS KING HAD GOTTEN HIS WAY, THERE WOULD BE NO CHRISTMAS. *WHO* WAS HE? **HEROD**

A MIRACULOUS STAR SHONE BRIGHTLY OVER THIS LITTLE TOWN. *WHERE* WAS IT? **BETHLEHEM**

IT'S ONE WAY WE RE-LIVE THE SPIRIT OF CHRISTMAS WITH LOVED ONES. *WHAT* IS IT? **GIFTS**

55

GNLEA — ANGEL
MRSISTHAC — CHRISTMAS
YMFALI — FAMILY
VROSAI — SAVIOR
NMGIDKO — KINGDOM
LKACB — BLACK
MIGA — MAGI
EUDAJ — JUDEA
TGSFI — GIFTS
LDGA — GLAD

58

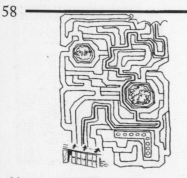

60

CA R V I N G

C O O K I N G

S K I I N G

T O B O G G A N

P H O N E

T R I M

CHRISTMAS IS ABOUT
G I V I N G
NOT GETTING.

61

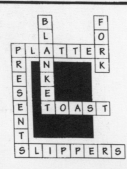

62

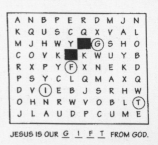

JESUS IS OUR **G I F T** FROM GOD.

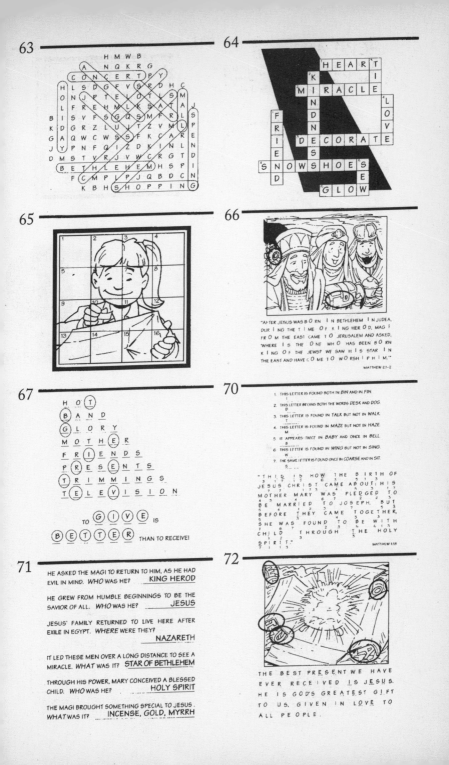

63

Word search with words: CONCERT, HOLIDAY, BELLS, GIFT, BETHLEHEM, SHOPPING, SPEND, etc.

64

Crossword:
HEART
KI
MIRACLE
KINDNESS
LOVE
FRIEND
DECORATE
SNOWSHOES
GLOW

65

66

"AFTER JESUS WAS BORN IN BETHLEHEM IN JUDEA, DURING THE TIME OF KING HEROD, MAGI FROM THE EAST CAME TO JERUSALEM AND ASKED, 'WHERE IS THE ONE WHO HAS BEEN BORN KING OF THE JEWS? WE SAW HIS STAR IN THE EAST AND HAVE COME TO WORSHIP HIM.'"

MATTHEW 2:1-2

67

HOT
BAND
GLORY
MOTHER
FRIENDS
PRESENTS
TRIMMINGS
TELEVISION

TO GIVE IS BETTER THAN TO RECEIVE!

70

1. THIS LETTER IS FOUND BOTH IN BIN AND IN FIN.
2. THIS LETTER BEGINS BOTH THE WORDS DESK AND DOG. D
3. THIS LETTER IS FOUND IN TALK BUT NOT IN WALK. T
4. THIS LETTER IS FOUND IN MAZE BUT NOT IN HAZE. M
5. IT APPEARS TWICE IN BABY AND ONCE IN BELL. B
6. THIS LETTER IS FOUND IN WING BUT NOT IN SING. W
7. THE SAME LETTER IS FOUND ONCE IN COARSE AND IN SIT. S

"THIS IS HOW THE BIRTH OF JESUS CHRIST CAME ABOUT: HIS MOTHER MARY WAS PLEDGED TO BE MARRIED TO JOSEPH, BUT BEFORE THEY CAME TOGETHER, SHE WAS FOUND TO BE WITH CHILD THROUGH THE HOLY SPIRIT."

MATTHEW 1:18

71

HE ASKED THE MAGI TO RETURN TO HIM, AS HE HAD EVIL IN MIND. *WHO* WAS HE? **KING HEROD**

HE GREW FROM HUMBLE BEGINNINGS TO BE THE SAVIOR OF ALL. *WHO* WAS HE? **JESUS**

JESUS' FAMILY RETURNED TO LIVE HERE AFTER EXILE IN EGYPT. *WHERE* WERE THEY? **NAZARETH**

IT LED THESE MEN OVER A LONG DISTANCE TO SEE A MIRACLE. *WHAT* WAS IT? **STAR OF BETHLEHEM**

THROUGH HIS POWER, MARY CONCEIVED A BLESSED CHILD. *WHO* WAS HE? **HOLY SPIRIT**

THE MAGI BROUGHT SOMETHING SPECIAL TO JESUS. *WHAT* WAS IT? **INCENSE, GOLD, MYRRH**

72

THE BEST PRESENT WE HAVE EVER RECEIVED IS JESUS. HE IS GOD'S GREATEST GIFT TO US, GIVEN IN LOVE TO ALL PEOPLE.

73

THE BEST PRESENT EVER.

THE KING OF THE JEWS.

NAZARETH, A TOWN IN GALILEE.

GLORY TO GOD IN THE HIGHEST.

THE ANGEL OF THE LORD.

74

75

GO	S T O P
BROTHER	S I S T E R
AUNT	U N C L E
WRAP	U N W R A P
BLACK	W H I T E
FULL	H U N G R Y
STAY	M O V E

A WELL KNOWN CHRISTMAS EVENT.

N A T I V I T Y

76

CWHTA	WATCH
EHLBTEMHE	BETHLEHEM
OYHL	HOLY
TRSA	STAR
VREALT	TRAVEL
NLPA	PLAN
TRAAZHEN	NAZARETH
EMRAD	DREAM
NRWSEA	ANSWER
HEOP	HOPE

77

IF EVERYONE PITCHES IN, ALL WILL HAVE A G R E A T DAY!

78

80

G A B

H O L Y

B R E A D

S K I I N G

M I R A C L E

N A T I V I T Y

C H O C O L A T E

GLORY TO GOD IN THE

H I G H E S T

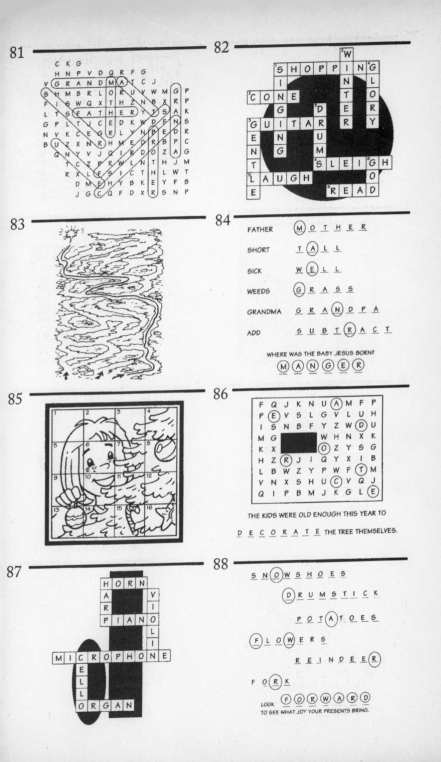

81

82

83

84

FATHER   Ⓜ O T H E R

SHORT   T A L L

SICK   W E L L

WEEDS   Ⓖ R A S S

GRANDMA G R A Ⓝ D P A

ADD   S U B T Ⓡ A C T

WHERE WAS THE BABY JESUS BORN?

Ⓜ Ⓐ Ⓝ Ⓖ Ⓔ Ⓡ

85

86

THE KIDS WERE OLD ENOUGH THIS YEAR TO

D E C O R A T E THE TREE THEMSELVES.

87

88

S N Ⓞ W S H O E S

Ⓓ R U M S T I C K

P O T Ⓐ T O E S

Ⓕ L Ⓞ W E R S

R E I N D E E Ⓡ

F O Ⓡ K

LOOK Ⓕ Ⓞ Ⓡ W Ⓐ Ⓡ Ⓓ

TO SEE WHAT JOY YOUR PRESENTS BRING.

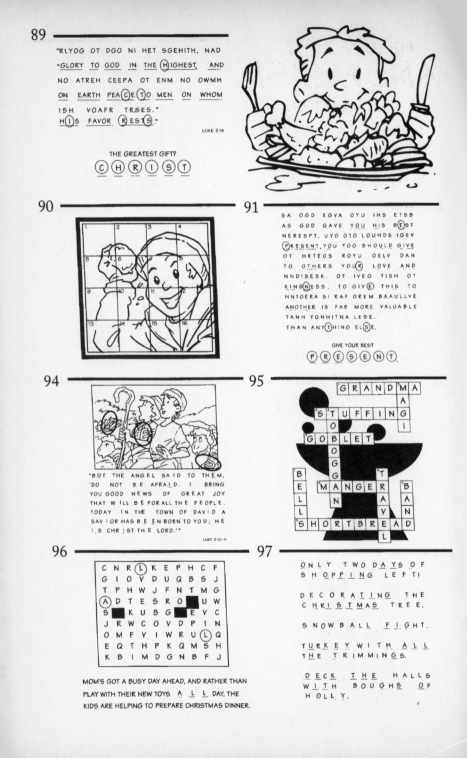

89

"RLYOG OT DGO NI HET SGEHITH, NAD
"GLORY TO GOD IN THE (H)IGHEST, AND
NO ATREH CEEPA OT ENM NO OWMH
ON EARTH PEA(C)E(T)O MEN ON WHOM
ISH VOAFR TRSES."
IS H VOAFR TRSES."
H(I)S FAVOR (R)ES(T)S."

LUKE 2:14

THE GREATEST GIFT?
(C) (H) (R) (I) (S) (T)

90

91

SA OGD EGVA OYU IHS ETSB
AS GOD GAVE Y(O)U HIS B(E)ST
NERESPT. UYO OTO LOUHDS IGEV
(P)RESENT. YOU TOO SHOULD GI(V)E
OT HRTEOS ROYU OELV DAN
TO OTHERS YOU(R) LOVE AND
NNDISESK. OT IVEG TISH OT
KIND(N)ESS. TO GIV(E) THIS TO
HNTOERA SI RAF OREM BAAULLVE
ANOTHER IS FAR MORE VALUABLE
TANH YGNHITNA LESE.
THAN ANY(T)HING EL(S)E.

GIVE YOUR BEST
(P) (R) (E) (S) (E) (N) (T)

94

"BUT THE ANGEL SAID TO TH(E)M,
'DO NOT B E AFRA I D. I BRING
YOU GOOD NEWS OF GREAT JOY
THAT W I LL B E FOR ALL TH E P E OPLE.
TODAY I N THE TOWN OF DAV I D A
SAV I OR HAS B E E N BORN TO YOU; HE
I S CHR I ST TH E LORD.'"

LUKE 2:10-11

95

G R A N D M A
S T U F F I N G
G O B L E T
B E L L   M A N G E R   B A N
S H O R T B R E A D

96

C N R (L) K E P H C F
G I O V D U Q B S J
T P H W J F N T M G
(A) D T E S R O U W
S K U B G E V C
J R W C O V D P I N
O M F V I W R U (L) Q
E Q T H P K Q M S H
K B I M D G N B F J

MOM'S GOT A BUSY DAY AHEAD, AND RATHER THAN
PLAY WITH THEIR NEW TOYS A L L DAY, THE
KIDS ARE HELPING TO PREPARE CHRISTMAS DINNER.

97

ONLY TWO DA Y S OF
S H OPP I NG LEFT!

DECORAT I NG THE
C H R I S T MAS TREE.

SNOWBALL F I GHT.

T U R K E Y WITH A L L
THE T R IMMING S.

D E C K T H E HALLS
WITH BOUGH S OF
HOLL Y.

HERE ARE THE ANSWERS!

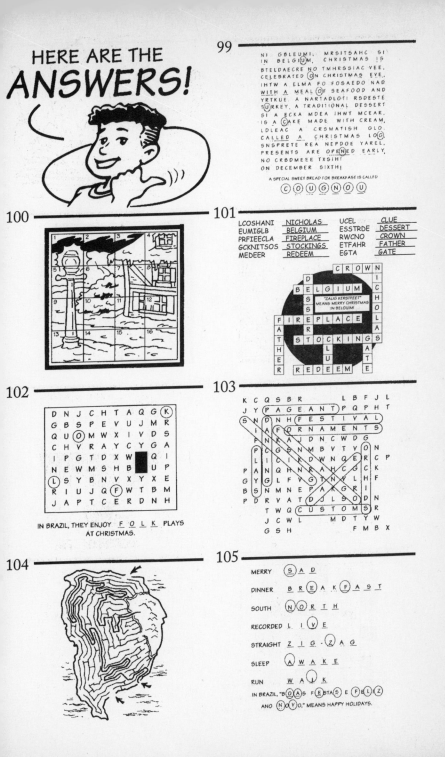

99

NI GBLEUMI, MRSITSAHC SI IN BELGIUM, CHRISTMAS IS BTELDAEGRE NO TMHRSSIAC VEE, CELEBRATED ON CHRISTMAS EVE. IHTW A ELMA FO FOSAEDO NAD WITH A MEAL OF SEAFOOD AND YRTKUE. A NARTADLOTI RSDESTE TURKEY. A TRADITIONAL DESSERT SI A ECKA MDEA IHWT MCEAR, IS A CAKE MADE WITH CREAM, LDLEAC A CRSMATISH GLO. CALLED A CHRISTMAS LOG. SNSPRETE REA NEPDOE YAREL, PRESENTS ARE OPENED EARLY, NO CRBDMEEE TXSIHT ON DECEMBER SIXTH!

A SPECIAL SWEET BREAD FOR BREAKFAST IS CALLED

C O U G N O U

101

LCOSHANI	NICHOLAS	UCEL	CLUE
EUMIGLB	BELGIUM	ESSTRDE	DESSERT
PRFIEECLA	FIREPLACE	RWCNO	CROWN
GCKNITSOS	STOCKINGS	ETFAHR	FATHER
MEDEER	REDEEM	EGTA	GATE

"ZALIG KERSTFEET" MEANS MERRY CHRISTMAS IN BELGUIMI

CROWN
BELGIUM
FIREPLACE
STOCKINGS
REDEEM

102

IN BRAZIL, THEY ENJOY F O L K PLAYS AT CHRISTMAS.

103

PAGEANT
FESTIVAL
ORNAMENTS
PLAYS
CUSTOMS

105

MERRY — S A D

DINNER — B R E A K F A S T

SOUTH — N O R T H

RECORDED — L I V E

STRAIGHT — Z I G - Z A G

SLEEP — A W A K E

RUN — W A L K

IN BRAZIL, "BOAS FESTAS E FELIZ ANO NOVO," MEANS HAPPY HOLIDAYS.

BOXING DAY IS THE BIG
CHRISTMAS CELEBRATION
IN ENGLAND AND IS A
NATIONAL HOLIDAY. BOXED
PRESENTS, PLACED IN CHURCHES
THROUGHOUT THE YEAR ARE
OPENED ON THIS DAY.

L E D
A C T S
B O X E D
S T O N E D
H O L I D A Y
N A T I O N A L
P R I N C I P L E

THIS DAY IS ALSO CALLED
SAINT S T E P H E N DAY,
AFTER THE CHRISTIAN MARTYR WHO WAS STONED
TO DEATH, AS TOLD IN THE BOOK OF ACTS.

E N I D J S B F G A
M K Q U G P W V M Q
C F W X A Q D S I
O J X L U M J H B
G V B H N T K W L X
S P U C O I G A O V
A N D J Q F W P V D
H K M X R S C L U F
L C P H O B K N I E

LEGEND TELLS US THAT IT WAS IN GERMANY WHERE
THE CHRISTMAS T R E E WAS SUPPOSEDLY
FIRST INTRODUCED.

THEY FIRST BEGAN TO BRING THESE INTO THEIR
HOMES. WHAT IS IT? ___CHRISTMAS TREE

HE WAS THE ONE BEHIND THE REFORMATION AND A
CHRISTMAS SYMBOL. WHO IS HE? MARTIN LUTHER

A HUGE TOY FAIR KICKS OFF CHRISTMAS IN THIS
COUNTRY. WHERE IS IT? ___GERMANY

GERMANS LOVE TO DECORATE AROUND A FRAME THAT
CAN BE SEEN OUTSIDE. WHAT IS IT? ___WINDOW

GERMANS LOVE TO HEAR THIS GROUP WHO VISIT
THEIR HOMES. WHO ARE THEY? ___CAROLERS

O TANNENBAUM.

THE ADVENT CALENDAR
IS A TRADITION IN
GERMANY.

IN GERMANY, POPULAR
TREATS ARE FIGURES MADE
OF SUGARY MARZIPAN
DOUGH.

TO SAY MERRY CHRISTMAS
IN GERMAN WOULD BE,
"FROEHLICHE WEINNACHTEN."

FOR CHILDREN, A TOY
FAIR IS THE BEST WAY
TO BEGIN CHRISTMAS.

IN THIS COUNTRY, THE SHORTEST, DARKEST DAY IS
DECEMBER 22. WHERE IS IT? ___SWEDEN

A SPECIAL MEAL IS EATEN ON THIS MOST IMPOR-
TANT DAY. WHAT DAY IS IT? CHRISTMAS EVE

IN SWEDEN, MANY GO HERE TO MEET ON CHRIST-
MAS MORNING. WHERE IS IT? ___CHURCH

BECAUSE OF WINTER DARKNESS, THESE ARE VERY
IMPORTANT. WHAT ARE THEY? ___CANDLES

KRINGLE, KRUMKAKE, AND SANDBAKKELS ARE
TRADITIONAL. WHAT ARE THEY? ___SWEETS

AN IMPORTANT FIGURE IN SWEDISH TRADITION WHO
WAS MARTYRED. WHO IS SHE? ___ST. LUCIA

115

116

BELIEF	D O U B T	
NIGHT	D A Y	
BLACK	W H I T E	
YOUNG	O L D	
FORWARD	B A C K W A R D	
SIT	S T A N D	
CROOKED	S T R A I G H T	

LONG AGO, A YOUNG SWEDISH GIRL WAS KILLED FOR HER CHRISTIAN BELIEFS AND IS NOW KNOWN AS S T. L U C I A SHE IS REMEMBERED ON DECEMBER 13, WHICH IS NOW A SPECIAL DAY IN THE SWEDISH CHRISTMAS.

117

118

1. THIS LETTER IS FOUND IN BOTH DRESS AND GET.
   E
2. IT'S FOUND ONCE IN ROBE AND TWICE IN RIBBON.
   B
3. FOUND FIRST IN BOTH CANDLES AND IN CANDY.
   C
4. FOUND FIRST IN BOTH FRANCE AND IN FRENCH.
   F
5. THIS LETTER BEGINS X-RAY AND ENDS BOX.
   X
6. THIS LETTER IS FOUND IN REST BUT NOT IN BEST.
   R

IN FRANCE, CHRISTMAS TREES ARE DECORATED WITH WHITE CANDLES AND RED RIBBONS. EVEN TREES OUTSIDE ARE DECORATED AND LIT THROUGH THE NIGHT. IN THE LANGUAGE OF THE FRENCH, ONE WOULD HEAR MERRY CHRISTMAS AS, "JOYEUX NOEL."

119

B O W
R O B E
B R E A D
W I N D O W
H O L I D A Y
P I C T U R E S
B E A U T I F U L

CANDLES AND R I B B O N S ARE A PART OF A FRENCH CHRISTMAS.

120

OESTH NI NADII HOW EAR FO THOSE IN INDIA WHO ARE OF HET THRNSIAIC TAHIF TECLERBAE THE CHRISTIAN FAITH CELEBRATE AITHMSSCR SA LELW. TYEH CHRISTMAS AS WELL. THEY OTREDECA HREIT HHCRUSCE IHWT DECORATE THEIR CHURCHES WITH A TBFLUEUIA WLFEOR ELALCD A BEAUTIFUL FLOWER CALLED HTE EITAPOSTIN NAD AGONM RO THE POINSETTIA AND MANGO OR BNAANA ESRET RAE LLUFOYLRCO BANANA TREES ARE COLORFULLY RTDNONEMEA. ORNAMENTED.

IN INDIA, C H A R I T Y IS CALLED, "BAKSHEESH."

121

FPTOORO	ROOFTOP	OYJ	JOY
TSNPEOAIIT	POINSETTIA	DNAII	INDIA
IASTELFV	FESTIVAL	ISFTG	GIFTS
NHDGTIMI	MIDNIGHT	SAMS	MASS
YRHACTI	CHARITY	WLLA	WALL
MIYFLA	FAMILY	TPO	POT

(crossword grid with answers: MASS, POT, INDIA, POINSETTIA, GIFT, CHARITY, FESTIVAL, JOY, FAMILY, etc.)

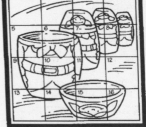

123

IN FINLAND, CHRISTMAS EVE, CHRISTMAS DAY, AND BOXING DAY ARE HELD TO BE THE THREE HOLY DAYS. CHRISTMAS DINNER IS CONSIDERED A FEAST AFTER A LIGHT BREAKFAST OF PLUM JUICE AND RICE PORRIDGE.

(crossword grid with answers: RADIO, HOUSE, TURKEY, CANDLE, plus down words)

(word search grid)

THE CHRISTMAS GREETING IN RUSSIA IS
"HRISTOS RAZDAJETSJA."

THE COLLAPSE OF THE SOVIET UNION.

THE RUSSIAN PEOPLE ARE FREE TO CELEBRATE CHRISTMAS.

CHRISTMAS IN RUSSIA IS CELEBRATED FOR TWELVE DAYS, FROM DECEMBER 25 TO JANUARY 5.

RUSSIAN CELEBRATIONS INCLUDE CIRCUSES, SPORTS, AND CARNIVALS.

(numbered puzzle illustration, pieces 1–15)

1. THIS LETTER BEGINS BOTH HEAR AND HERE. H
2. THIS LETTER ENDS BOTH BLOCK AND BLACK. K
3. THIS LETTER IS FOUND IN CAST BUT NOT IN LAST. C
4. IT ENDS THE WORD CAT AND BEGINS THE WORD TOY. T
5. IT APPEARS TWICE IN SOON AND ONCE IN HOT. O
6. IT'S FOUND ONCE IN FIVE AND TWICE IN VALVE. V
7. THIS LETTER IS FOUND IN GIFT BUT NOT IN RIFT. G
8. THIS LETTER BEGINS BOTH BLOCK AND BLACK. B

CHRISTIANS IN HONG KONG HAVE ADAPTED THE CHRISTMAS CELEBRATION INTO AN EASTERN SETTING. NATIVITY SCENES AND CHRISTMAS CARDS HAVE A CHINESE LOOK AND ARE VERY ARTISTIC.

(word search grid)

130

IDEOGRAPH
HONGKONG
STREAMERS
CHINESE
CHAINS
CHURCHES

131

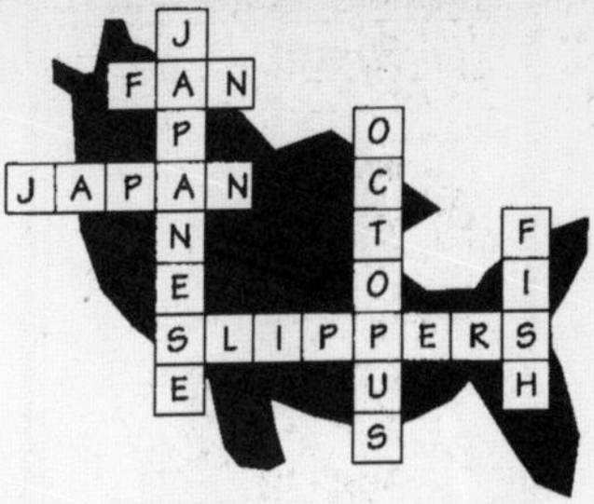
JAPANESE
FAN
JAPAN
OCTOPUS
FISH
SLIPPERS

132

WEST E (A) S T

WATER L A (N) D

SHOES S L I (P) P E R S

ADULT (J) U V E N I L E

SOFT H (A) R D

CAN YOU PRONOUNCE THE CHRISTMAS GEETING IN (J)(A)(P)(A)(N): "SHINNEN OMEDETO, KURISUMASU OMEDETO"? *WOW!*

133

D	R	W	A	R	K	Z	V	A	J
J	T	X	Z	J	W	T	P	I	X
L	D	V	Y	D	G	F	S	K	H
Q	M	F	X	Q	S	(U)	C	T	V
E	S	W	L	C	H	R	G	E	R
H	P	J	I	P	Q	A	I	(N)	M
A	V	M	M	L	X	Y	V	M	Q
K	(B)	C	E	W	S	F	Z	D	S
G	I	K	H	E	Z	P	Y	R	M
F	G	Y	T	C	L	(O)	J	H	A

"B U O N NATALE" IS HOW YOU SAY MERRY CHRISTMAS IN ITALY.

134

CHILDREN HOPE THAT "GESÚ BAMBINO" WILL BRING THEM GIFTS. *WHO* IS HE? BABY JESUS

"PRESEPIO" IS AN ITALIAN NAME FOR A FAMILIAR CHRISTMAS SCENE. *WHAT* IS IT? NATIVITY

THESE ARE SPECIAL "BAGS" THAT MEN MAKE MUSIC ON. *WHAT* ARE THEY? BAGPIPES

IN ITALY, ONLY THIS MEAT IS EATEN ON THE FAST AT CHRISTMAS EVE. *WHAT* IS IT? FISH

NO ITALIAN MEAL CAN BE COMPLETE WITHOUT THIS TRADITIONAL DISH. *WHAT* IS IT? PASTA

MUSICIANS DRESS IN SHEEPSKIN JACKETS AS A REMINDER OF THESE WHO WERE PRESENT AT CHRIST'S BIRTH. *WHO* ARE THEY? SHEPHERDS

135

137

NI PINAS, THMSSCRIA EEV SI
IN SPAIN, CHRISTMAS EVE IS
OLAS ONWNK SA ETH GTNIH FO
A(L)SO KNOWN AS THE NIGHT OF
DOGO ITDIGNS. A IILNARDATTO
GOOD TIDINGS. A (T)RADITIONAL
MAGE SI EON HEWER DRIHCELN
GAME IS O(N)E WHE(R)E CHILDREN
HTI TA A RETE RNUKT LFLU
HIT AT A TRE(E) TRUNK FULL
FO IOODGSE, IRNGTY OT ONCKK
OF GOODI(E)S, TRYING T(O) KNOCK
ETMH UTO.
THEM (O)UT.

SPAIN HAS A LEGEND OF A COAL MINER, NAMED (O)(L)(E)(N)(T) Z(E)(R)(O) WHO CAME DOWN FROM A MOUNTAIN TO ANNOUNCE THE BIRTH OF CHRIST.

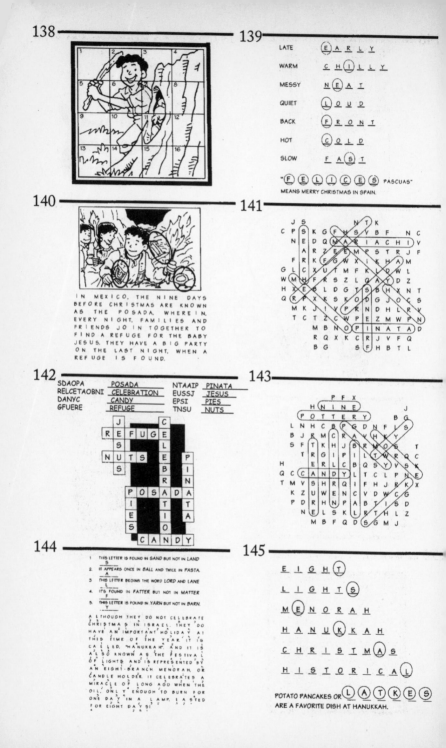

138

139

LATE — E A R L Y

WARM — C H I L L Y

MESSY — N E A T

QUIET — L O U D

BACK — F R O N T

HOT — C O L D

SLOW — F A S T

"F E L I C E S PASCUAS" MEANS MERRY CHRISTMAS IN SPAIN.

140

IN MEXICO, THE NINE DAYS BEFORE CHRISTMAS ARE KNOWN AS THE POSADA, WHEREIN, EVERY NIGHT, FAMILIES AND FRIENDS JOIN TOGETHER TO FIND A REFUGE FOR THE BABY JESUS. THEY HAVE A BIG PARTY ON THE LAST NIGHT, WHEN A REFUGE IS FOUND.

141

142

SDAOPA — POSADA
RELCETAOBNI — CELEBRATION
DANYC — CANDY
GFUERE — REFUGE
NTAAIP — PINATA
EUSSJ — JESUS
EPSI — PIES
TNSU — NUTS

143

144

1. THIS LETTER IS FOUND IN SAND BUT NOT IN LAND — S
2. IT APPEARS ONCE IN BALL AND TWICE IN PASTA — A
3. THIS LETTER BEGINS THE WORD LORD AND LANE — L
4. IT'S FOUND IN FATTER BUT NOT IN MATTER — F
5. THIS LETTER IS FOUND IN YARN BUT NOT IN BARN — Y

ALTHOUGH THEY DO NOT CELEBRATE CHRISTMAS IN ISRAEL, THEY DO HAVE AN IMPORTANT HOLIDAY AT THIS TIME OF THE YEAR. IT IS CALLED "HANUKKAH", AND IT IS ALSO KNOWN AS THE FESTIVAL OF LIGHTS AND IS REPRESENTED BY AN EIGHT-BRANCH MENORAH, OR CANDLE HOLDER. IT CELEBRATES A MIRACLE OF LONG AGO WHEN THE OIL, ONLY ENOUGH TO BURN FOR ONE DAY IN A LAMP, LASTED FOR EIGHT DAYS!

145

E I G H T

L I G H T S

M E N O R A H

H A N U K K A H

C H R I S T M A S

H I S T O R I C A L

POTATO PANCAKES OR L A T K E S ARE A FAVORITE DISH AT HANUKKAH.

146

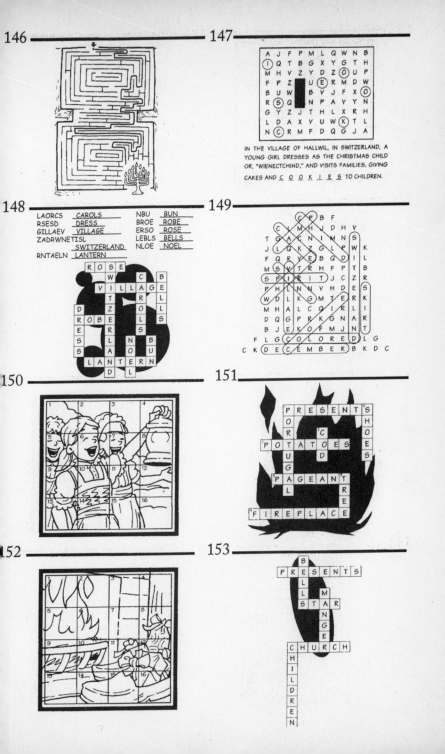

147

A	J	F	P	M	L	Q	W	N	B
I	Q	T	B	G	X	Y	G	T	H
M	H	V	Z	Y	D	Z	O	U	P
F	P	Z			U	E	R	M	D	W
B	U	W			B	V	J	F	X	O
R	S	Q			N	P	A	V	Y	N
G	Y	Z	J	T	H	L	X	R	H
L	D	A	X	V	U	W	K	T	L
N	C	R	M	F	D	Q	G	J	A

IN THE VILLAGE OF HALLWIL, IN SWITZERLAND, A YOUNG GIRL DRESSES AS THE CHRISTMAS CHILD OR, "WIENECTCHIND," AND VISITS FAMILIES, GIVING CAKES AND C O O K I E S TO CHILDREN.

148

LAORCS — CAROLS
RSESD — DRESS
GILLAEV — VILLAGE
ZADRWNETISL — SWITZERLAND
RNTAELN — LANTERN

NBU — BUN
BROE — ROBE
ERSO — ROSE
LEBLS — BELLS
NLOE — NOEL

149

150

151

152

153

HERE ARE THE
ANSWERS!

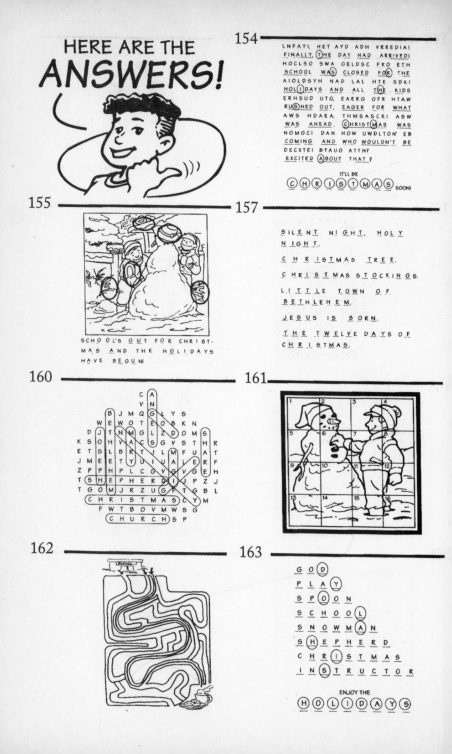

154

LNFAYI HET AYD ADH VRREDIAI
FINALLY, THE DAY HAD ARRIVED!
HOCLSO SWA OELDSC FRO ETH
SCHOOL WAS CLOSED FOR THE
AIOLDSYH NAD LAL HTE SDKI
HOLIDAYS AND ALL THE KIDS
ERHSUD UTO, EAERG OFR HTAW
RUSHED OUT, EAGER FOR WHAT
AWS HDAEA. THMSASCRI ASW
WAS AHEAD. CHRISTMAS WAS
NOMGCI DAN HOW UWDLTON' EB
COMING AND WHO WOULDN'T BE
DECXTEI BTAUO ATTH?
EXCITED ABOUT THAT?

IT'LL BE
(C)(H)(R)(I)(S)(T)(M)(A)(S) SOON!

155

SCHOOL'S OUT FOR CHRIST-
MAS AND THE HOLIDAYS
HAVE BEGUN!

157

SILENT NIGHT, HOLY
NIGHT.

CHRISTMAS TREE.

CHRISTMAS STOCKINGS.

LITTLE TOWN OF
BETHLEHEM.

JESUS IS BORN.

THE TWELVE DAYS OF
CHRISTMAS.

160

161

162

163

G O (D)
P L A (Y)
S P (O) O N
S C H O O (L)
S N O W (M) A N
(S) H E P H E R D
(C) H R I S T (M) A S
I N S T R U C T O R

ENJOY THE
(H)(O)(L)(I)(D)(A)(Y)(S)

164

THIS MAN HAS A LOT TO TEACH YOU IF YOU SHOW UP ONCE A WEEK. *WHO* IS HE? __PASTOR__

HE'LL SHOW YOU HOW TO GET DOWN THE MOUNTAIN SAFELY. *WHO* IS HE? __SKI INSTRUCTOR__

IT DOESN'T FLY AND IT MAKES YOUR MOUTH WATER EVERY YEAR. *WHAT* IS IT? __TURKEY__

IT IS VERY DIFFICULT WAITING TO FIND OUT THE CONTENTS OF THIS. *WHAT* IS IT? __GIFT__

AT THIS TIME OF YEAR, YOU'RE THINKING OF WHAT IS AHEAD. *WHERE* ARE YOU? __SCHOOL__

165

```
D J F O A M B L Q (U)
C I X P S Y P G N E
K M (R) N K E B V W X
G P S W D   Q C J
N L Q O B (T) F W N D
F A Y I G C S I M V
O C X K Y P J L A K
J W (H) V E Y X O V Q
A E S I M L B G D F
```

SNOWBALL FIGHTS ARE A LOT OF FUN, BUT TRY NOT TO H _U_ _R_ _T_ ANYONE!

167

Crossword with answers:
CHRISTMAS, CONCERTS, FORT, FRUITCAKE, CAROL, LOG, SPRITE, SNOWBOARD, JESUS, ICE

168

ERTE	TREE
KURTYE	TURKEY
ENKTANSOM	ORNAMENTS
NSRTEPP	PRESENT
HHJBFTELME	BETHLEHEM
IANSGGTK	SKATING

Crossword with answers: ORNAMENTS, SKATING, PRESENT, BETHLEHEM, TURKEY, TREE

169

1. BEGINS THE WORD NUT AND ENDS THE WORD MOON.
   N
2. APPEARS ONCE IN ICE AND TWICE IN SKIIS.
   I
3. THIS LETTER IS FOUND IN BEGAN BUT NOT IN BEGUN.
   A
4. APPEARS TWICE IN BOOT BUT ONLY ONCE IN POLE.
   O
5. FOUND TWICE IN BOTH SNOWSHOE AND SOCKS.
   S
6. YOU'LL FIND THIS IN LESS BUT NOT IN LOSS.
   E
7. BEGINS TREE AND IS IN THE MIDDLE OF MOTOR.
   T
8. APPEARS ONCE IN SISTER AND TWICE IN BROTHER.
   R

"YOU WILL BE WITH CHILD AND GIVE BIRTH TO A SON. AND YOU ARE TO GIVE HIM THE NAME JESUS."

170

SNOW	R A I (N)
UP	D O W (N)
RECEIVE	(G) I V E
DARK	L (I) G H T
FULL	E (M) P T Y
HAPPY	S (A) D
SISTER	B R O T H (E) R

CHRIST, THE TRUE
M E A N I N G
OF CHRISTMAS.

171

ON NLBAOLWS GTIHF SI EOPMLETC
NO SNOWBALL (F)IGHT IS COMPLETE

HTUTOIW A NRFWOOTS OT RERTATE
WITHOUT A SNO(W)FORT TO RETREAT

OT DAN EIHD NI. KMAE SA YANM
TO AND HIDE IN. MAKE AS MANY

OSWN CRKISB SA DENEDE DAN
SNOW BRICK(S) AS (N)EEDED AND

TCAKS HMTE NO AHEC ORHET, KIGANM
STACK THEM ON EACH (O)THER, MAKING

SREU HET ITNSOJ REA GGDTSREAE.
SURE (T)HE JOINTS ARE STAGGE(R)ED,

U'YLOL EB BVNCEIINLI!
YOU'LL BE INVINCIBLE!

YOU'LL NEED A
S N O W F O R T

175

T H E   T H R E E   W I S E   M E N.

T U R K E Y   W I T H   A L L   T H E
T R I M M I N G S.

C H R I S T,   T H E   S A V I O R,
I S   B O R N.

I T 'S   B E T T E R   T O   G I V E
T H A N   T O   R E C E I V E.

C H R I S T M A S   E V E.

M E R R Y   C H R I S T M A S   A N D
A   H A P P Y   N E W   Y E A R!

176

T O B O G G A N

S N O W F O R T

S N O W M O B I L E

I C E F I S H I N G

D R U M

S N O W M A N

WHAT'S REALLY, REALLY BIG AND COVERED WITH SNOW?
M O U N T A I N

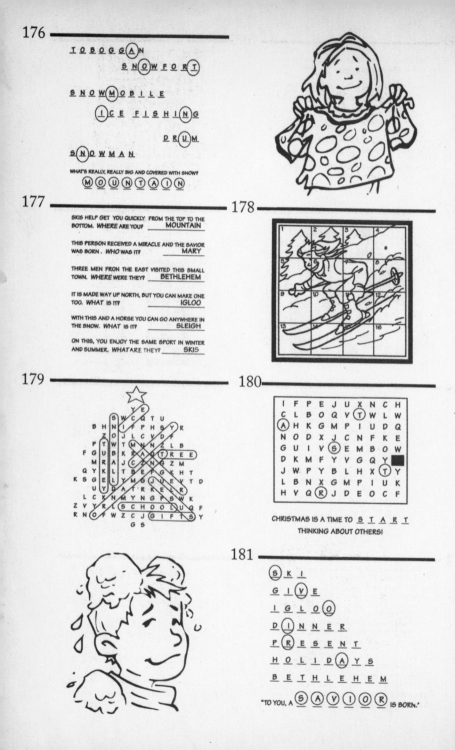

177

SKIS HELP GET YOU QUICKLY FROM THE TOP TO THE
BOTTOM. *WHERE ARE YOU?*   MOUNTAIN

THIS PERSON RECEIVED A MIRACLE AND THE SAVIOR
WAS BORN. *WHO WAS IT?*   MARY

THREE MEN FROM THE EAST VISITED THIS SMALL
TOWN. *WHERE WERE THEY?*   BETHLEHEM

IT IS MADE WAY UP NORTH, BUT YOU CAN MAKE ONE
TOO. *WHAT IS IT?*   IGLOO

WITH THIS AND A HORSE YOU CAN GO ANYWHERE IN
THE SNOW. *WHAT IS IT?*   SLEIGH

ON THIS, YOU ENJOY THE SAME SPORT IN WINTER
AND SUMMER. *WHAT ARE THEY?*   SKIS

178

179

180

CHRISTMAS IS A TIME TO S T A R T
THINKING ABOUT OTHERS!

181

S K I

G I V E

I G L O O

D I N N E R

P R E S E N T

H O L I D A Y S

B E T H L E H E M

"TO YOU, A S A V I O R IS BORN."

184

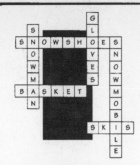

```
            G
      S     L
S N O W S H O E S
      O     V     N
      W     E     O
      M           W
B A S K E T       M
      N           O
                  B
            S K I S
                  L
                  E
```

185

186

YVNREOEE ELVOS ICVEGERIN
EVERYONE <u>LOVES</u> <u>RECE(I)VING</u>
FTIGS TA MRAHCTSSI NDA MEOS
<u>GIFTS</u> AT CHR(I)STMAS AND SO(M)E
VEHA NVEE ROSEEDVCDI HET OYJ
HAVE <u>EVE(N)</u> DISCOVERED THE <u>JOY</u>
AHTT MESCO NI NIIGVG SGFTI.
THAT <u>COME(S)</u> IN GIVING GIFTS.
IHTS TUSMOC SI EASDB NO
<u>THIS</u> CUSTOM IS BAS(E)D ON
GTFIS GOBRUTH OT HTE OWBENRN
GIFTS <u>BROUGHT</u> <u>TO</u> THE NE(W)BORN
EUSJS.
<u>JESUS.</u>

(W)(I)(S)(E) (M)(E)(N) OR MAGI,
KINGS FROM THE EAST, CARRIED GIFTS FOR THE LORD.

188

189

SICK	<u>H</u> E A <u>L</u> T(H)Y
RUN	(W) <u>A L K</u>
BUY	(S) <u>E L L</u>
UNWRAP	W (R)A P
TEACH	L E A R (N)
FAST	S L (O) <u>W</u>
SHRINK	G R (O) W
LAST	(F) <u>I R S T</u>

A PLACE OF REFUGE:
(S) (N)(O)(W) (F)(O)(R)(T)

192

```
B H Q I P C K R D S
S J N U D (L) N F I A
D W A S X Y U W T N
M P K G H B S M (E) K
Q ■ F X C J P Y C X
C Q N Y T G H W Q
G U M X F W A R J B
R A T J U I P Y (V) R
M (O) I G H B T D F K
```

JESUS WAS BORN BECAUSE OF GOD'S LOVE FOR
YOU! IN HIM, YOU TOO CAN <u>L O V E</u> OTHERS.

193

<u>T</u> H E <u>L</u> I <u>T</u> T <u>L</u> E <u>D</u> R <u>U</u> M M E <u>R</u>
<u>B</u> O Y.

<u>S</u> T A <u>R</u> O F <u>B</u> E T H L <u>E</u> H <u>E</u> M.

<u>P</u> E A <u>C</u> E <u>O</u> N <u>E</u> A <u>R</u> T H A <u>N</u> D
<u>G</u> O O <u>D</u> W I <u>L</u> L <u>T</u> O <u>M</u> E N.

<u>A</u> <u>B</u> A B Y <u>L</u> Y <u>I</u> N G <u>I</u> N <u>A</u>
M A N <u>G</u> E R.

<u>W</u> H <u>I</u> T E <u>C</u> H <u>R</u> I <u>S</u> T <u>M</u> A <u>S.</u>

194

1. IT CAN BE FOUND IN LAST BUT NOT IN LOST.
    A
2. LOOK FOR IT ONCE IN BOTH TOY AND IN YELL.
    Y
3. THIRD IN PLACE IN BOTH RENT AND IN LENT.
    N
4. IT CAN BE FOUND IN SONG BUT NOT IN SANG.
    O
5. IT DOUBLES BOTH BOOTS AND TOBOGANS.
    O
6. THIS LETTER BEGINS ROUND AND ENDS HOUR.
    R
7. IT IS FOUND AT THE BEGINNING OF JAM AND JOY.
    J

"WHEN THEY SAW THE STAR,
THEY WERE OVERJOYED. ON
COMING TO THE HOUSE, THEY
SAW THE CHILD WITH HIS MOTHER
MARY, AND THEY BOWED DOWN
AND WORSHIPED HIM"

MATTHEW 2:10-11

195

196

HOLLY
PRESENT
TREE
ORNAMENT
WREATH
SNOWBALL
TURKEY
BETHLEHEM

LITTLE TOWN OF DAVID.

197

MIRHSTCAS 51 05 CMHU FNU
CHRISTMAS IS SO MUCH FUN
NAD EYRVE ERYA VAEESL IGSTNAL
AND EVERY YEAR LEAVES LASTING
ERSIMMOE. PGEINKE NI DIMN. OT
MEMORIES. KEEPING IN MIND TO
EB NCOTREAIEDS OT OTESH
BE CONSIDERATE TO THOSE
NRAODU OYU SALVEE UYO HWTI
AROUND YOU LEAVES YOU WITH
MMOEESIR FO A RVYE ICPEASL
MEMORIES OF A VERY SPECIAL
IDKN.
KIND.

A BLESSED CHRISTMAS IS IN BEING KIND TO
OTHERS

198

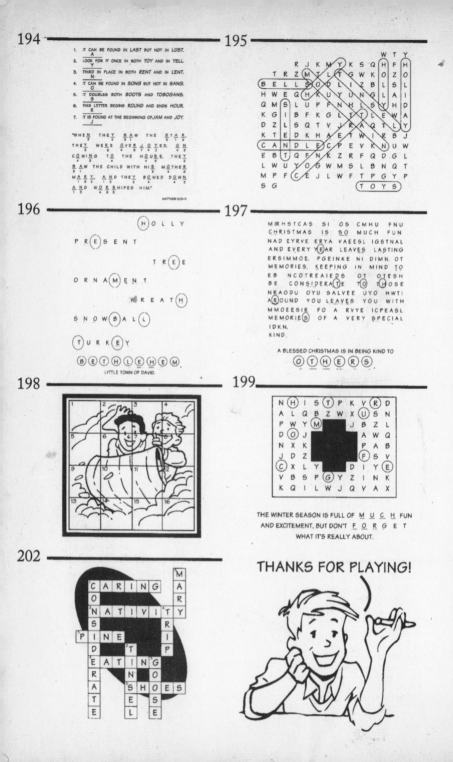

199

THE WINTER SEASON IS FULL OF M U C H FUN
AND EXCITEMENT, BUT DON'T F O R G E T
WHAT IT'S REALLY ABOUT.

202

THANKS FOR PLAYING!